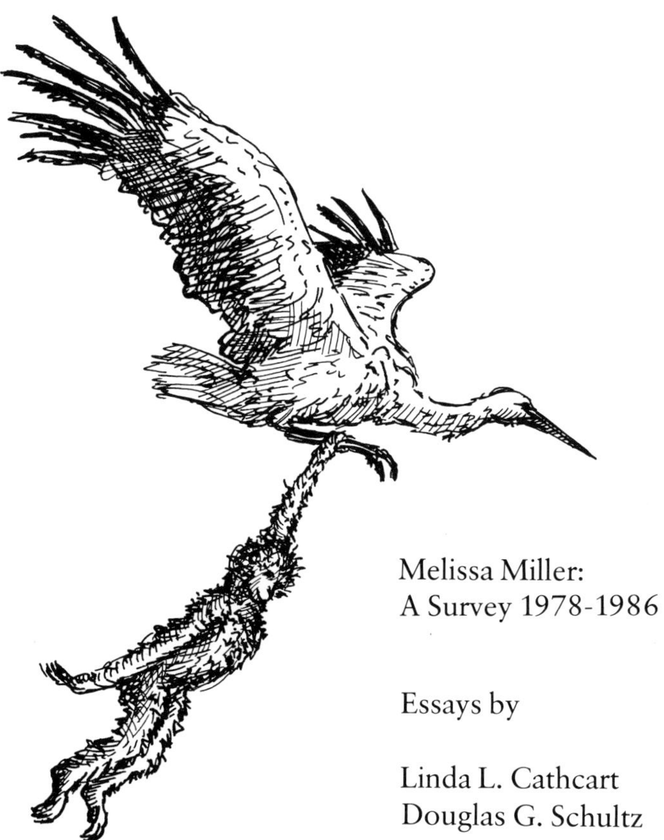

Melissa Miller:
A Survey 1978-1986

Essays by

Linda L. Cathcart
Douglas G. Schultz

Contemporary Arts Museum, Houston, Texas

This exhibition was organized by the Contemporary Arts Museum, Houston, Texas, in cooperation with the Albright-Knox Art Gallery, Buffalo, New York.

Exhibition Schedule

Albright-Knox Art Gallery
Buffalo, New York
July 12-August 24, 1986

Contemporary Arts Museum
Houston, Texas
September 13-November 3, 1986

The Fort Worth Art Museum
Fort Worth, Texas
November 24, 1986-January 4, 1987

Melissa Miller: A Survey 1978-1986 is funded through a grant from the National Endowment for the Arts with additional support from the Shell Companies Foundation, Incorporated, Arthur Andersen & Co., Mr. and Mrs. S. Maurice McAshan, Jr. and InterFirst Bank Houston.

The catalogue is funded through the *Contemporary Arts Publication Fund* established with the generous support of The Charles Engelhard Foundation in May 1982, with additional support in 1985-1986 from Tenneco Inc. and Mr. and Mrs. Meredith J. Long.

This exhibition is a project of TexArt/150, an association of art museums in Texas committed to celebrating the sesquicentennial anniversary through exhibitions and special programs. TexArt/150 projects are made possible in part by grants from Frito-Lay, Inc., the Atlantic Richfield Foundation, Texas Monthly Magazine and the Texas Commission on the Arts.

Contents

Melissa Miller: A Survey 1978-1986 is the third in a series of three exhibitions organized by the Contemporary Arts Museum in recognition of Texas' 150th birthday. The first in the series was *Robert Rauschenberg, Work from Four Series* and the second was *Joseph Glasco 1948-1986.* The idea that Texas museums should in some way participate in the celebration of Texas' sesquicentennial began to take shape in 1983 and, as a result TexArt/150, an umbrella organization, was created. It was under this organization's patronage that the Contemporary Arts Museum's idea to organize exhibitions to celebrate Texas' 150th birthday came to fruition.

Concomitant with the CAM's wish to honor Texas on the occasion of its 150th birthday, is the desire to show the art of our time, and the three shows in this series of sesquicentennial exhibitions fulfill that desire. Miller, a Texan born in Houston in 1951, is the youngest of the three artists included. First introduced in the Museum's *Perspectives* series exhibitions in 1981, she was selected to conclude this series of sesquicentennial exhibitions because it may be said that she represents Texas' future.

The Houston community has consistently demonstrated its support of exhibitions of this nature. We are deeply grateful to the Texas Commission on the Arts which has provided continuous sponsorship of our exhibition programs since 1979, and whose funds helped make this exhibition possible. From our community also come the gifts which support the *Contemporary Arts Publication Fund,* established by The Charles Engelhard Foundation in May 1982, with additional support in 1985-1986 from Tenneco Inc. and Mr. and Mrs. Meredith J. Long. This fund makes possible the handsome and scholarly publications which accompany our exhibitions. The *Visiting Artists Lecture Series Fund,* established by Mr. and Mrs. Fayez Sarofim and Fayez Sarofim and Co. in 1981, and increased in 1983, sponsors the lecture series program which has enabled the museum to bring all exhibiting artists and many art historians to Houston to talk in gallery tours and other programs which are free and open to the public. The Institute of Museum Services, a federal agency which contributes operating support to the nation's museums, has also helped to make our ambitious exhibition programs possible by providing funds for salaries.

We are also able to present this survey because of a generous grant from the National Endowment for the Arts. To match this grant, the Shell Companies Foundation, Incorporated, Arthur Andersen & Co., Mr. and Mrs. S. Maurice McAshan, Jr. and InterFirst Bank Houston have made special gifts to support this exhibition. We would also like to thank the Atlantic Richfield Foundation for their contribution which has enabled us to publish a *Children's Guide to Seeing,* authored by Phoebe Fleming, for the exhibition.

We are joined in this presentation by the Albright-Knox Art Gallery in Buffalo, New York, one of America's oldest museums, but with an eye always to future developments in art. In Buffalo this exhibition will be one of three representing new talent. The show is also being presented at the Fort Worth Art Museum, Texas. We extend our thanks to directors Douglas G. Schultz and E.A. Carmean for their interest in and enthusiasm for this show.

Lenders to the exhibition include not only major museums and corporations, to whom we are very grateful, but private collectors as well, many of whom have followed Miller's promising career over the years. It is not possible to say how much their generosity in lending their paintings is appreciated.

Foreword

This catalogue, we hope, will be a meaningful accompaniment to this exhibition and will serve as a useful reference tool to future curators and researchers. We are very pleased to include a most thoughtful and perceptive essay by Douglas G. Schultz on the important role animals play in Miller's work. Mr. Schultz was ably and patiently assisted by his Editor for Special Projects, Karen Lee Spaulding; Kathryn L. Schenck, Assistant Librarian; and Ida Koch, his Secretary.

Thanks must go to the entire staff of the Contemporary Arts Museum. Hannah Baker, Curatorial Assistant, tirelessly and cheerfully assisted me in the organization and implementation of both the exhibition and catalogue, and Lou Cinda Holt, Registrar, carefully and diligently saw to the coordination of the loans. Cheryl Blissitte and Emily Todd patiently saw the exhibition catalogue through many refinements, and everyone on the staff lent their support and expertise in all phases of the exhibition's creation.

We also want to thank long-time friends of the Contemporary Arts Museum, Fredericka Hunter and Ian Glennie of Texas Gallery, as well as their Assistant Director Kathleen Crain, without whose assistance this exhibition would not have been possible. Miller's dealer in New York, Holly Solomon, and her assistant Sam Pratt, must also be thanked for quickly and willingly providing much information and material for this catalogue.

Many museums, galleries and libraries contributed indispensable assistance to our research efforts. Honey Harrison, Hirsch Library, The Museum of Fine Arts, Houston, and Violet Johnson of the Houston Public Library, as usual were especially helpful. Special thanks are extended to those who generously loaned color separations for reproduction purposes: Cathy Marcus and *Texas Monthly* Magazine; Prudence Carlson and *Art in America*; J. Tolnick and the Bell Gallery, Brown University, Providence; Lisa Doolittle and Tilden-Foley Gallery, New Orleans; and Phyllis Rosenzweig and the Hirshhorn Museum and Sculpture Garden, Washington, D.C. We would also like to thank Terry Hildebrand, Director of the Sarah Campbell Blaffer Foundation, Houston, for kindly allowing us to reproduce the work from their collection. We also extend thanks to Robert Mapplethorpe who granted us permission to reproduce his photograph of the artist.

Finally, it has been a joy working with the artist and her family who were always available to answer questions and offer enthusiastic support for the show. It is indeed an honor to include Melissa Miller in this series of exhibitions celebrating Texas' birthday!

Linda L. Cathcart

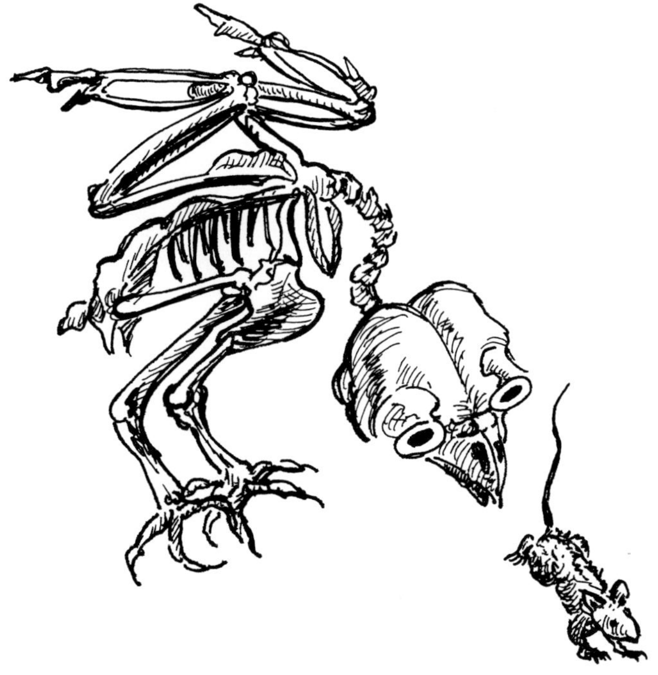

**Observation, Anticipation and Temptation
in the Paintings of Melissa Miller**
Linda L. Cathcart

Melissa Miller grew up in Houston, Texas, the second of four children born to two native fourth-generation Texans. One of three daughters, Miller had an early childhood that was rich in playtime with her siblings. Each summer, the family packed up and went to her maternal grandfather's cabin near Las Vegas, New Mexico, in the Sangre de Cristo mountains, to escape the Houston heat and to pay a very traditional visit. The children and their cousins spent the summers in the canyons and forests, fishing, hiking and picnicking, playing with the domesticated animals, as well as observing the wild ones. In New Mexico and Texas, Miller first observed the dramatic weather changes which appear in her early pictures.

When Miller was eleven, she began to split the summers between time in New Mexico and camp in Kerrville, Texas. Her camp, an old and traditional one, stressed the values she had learned at church—patience, loyalty, family devotion, giving—but also added to her values independence and the idea of competition.

During the school year, Miller's family spent every weekend at her paternal grandfather's small ranch in Flatonia, Texas—about halfway between Houston and Austin. As at the New Mexico cabin, dogs, cats and chickens were playmates to the children, who also had many pets at home—dogs, cats, fish and birds.

After graduating from high school in 1969, Miller joined a group called Amigos de las Américas and spent the summer in Guatemala. The students administered vaccinations to the local population of Sanarate, something they were barely equipped to do. For Miller, who had rarely traveled outside of Texas—and then only with family—this was an important challenge and it gave her her first adult sense that landscapes and peoples varied a great deal from place to place.

In 1969, Miller entered college at The University of Texas at Austin with the idea, after the Guatemala experience, that she might become a nurse or an anthropologist. Almost accidentally, she signed up for some art classes and found them of importance to her. Prior to college, her experiences with art had been limited to the structured, creative times at school and camp and the usual exposure of a child whose family participates in civic affairs and frequents public institutions and events. Her most important exposure was a trip to New York, when she was about nineteen, which included The Museum of Modern Art and The Metropolitan Museum of Art. At the Modern, she saw the impressive Monet *Water Lilies*, 1920, paintings. After two years at UT, Miller came home and spent a year at the Museum of Fine Arts School in Houston (now the Alfred C. Glassell School of Art). She cites this experience as a significant one because the artists who were her teachers were practically her own age and for the first time, she was totally immersed in art as an exclusive activity. Her first independent efforts were abstract paintings.

In 1972, ready for a change, Miller applied to The University of New Mexico in Albuquerque, mostly because she admired the landscape and was familiar with the location from family trips. The art department was a strong one and Miller spent most of her time absorbing the lessons of Abstract Expressionism taught by her instructors. She also made friends who were politically active—many with various labor causes. Because of these influences, she assumed that when she graduated she would probably support herself by working in a factory. Instead, her professors nominated her to Yale University Summer School of Music and Art, Norfolk, Connecticut, and she was accepted. During the summer of 1974 at Yale, she finished the credits necessary for a Bachelor's Degree in Fine Arts and did not return to The University of New Mexico.

It was at The University of New Mexico that Miller learned the basic processes which she continues to use as a painter. She never learned to make preliminary sketches for paintings because she found it more exciting to work freely at the canvas, rather than transfer a small drawing to the larger canvas. Her compositions are made directly on the canvas— each mark feeds from the marks which have previously been made, letting painterly gestures play off against one another and develop into a painting. She learned the Abstract Expressionists' thesis that while there might be certain themes, directions or goals for a painting at its beginning, its final appearance is determined by the interplay of material on the surface of the canvas.

Yale was a powerful influence on Miller's decision to be an artist. The school was very serious and competitive, and for the first time, she realized that one could be a fine artist, and that being an artist could be an actual profession. Besides her classes, Miller was thrilled by the visiting artist program which brought artists like Philip Guston, who would become a special favorite, and painters who were women, such as Joan Snyder, to campus to speak. In the library, she looked at reproductions in art books—particularly on the Fauves—and she painted landscapes which drew upon earlier lessons of Abstract Expressionism, combined with new influences. Gabriel Laderman, whose beautiful, serene paintings are very realistic, was her professor; she remembers the school as being split between those who painted figuratively and those who pursued abstraction. Miller's own paintings acknowledged many sources. She painted large brightly-colored landscapes which she says were really dominated by color fields in which she could paint abstractly "like Diebenkorn."[1] These landscapes included realistically rendered buildings. At this time, Miller also became familiar with the work of Charles Burchfield. Like Thomas Hart Benton, whose work—particularly his landscapes—she had already admired, Burchfield had chosen to be a regionalist artist. Miller now had the ability to consider many choices concerning her artistic career.

After completing her Bachelor's degree, Miller spent the fall hitch-hiking alone across the United States, along the California coastline and finally home to Texas—stopping at important museums, such as the Philadelphia, Boston, Cleveland and San Francisco museums, along the way. When she returned to Texas it was 1975, and she decided to live at the family ranch in Flatonia. Her elderly grandfather had died and Miller was alone with the landscape and the animals and her painting. This situation provided her with a subject matter all her own; now she had a real landscape to paint, one that she knew well, had strong emotional ties to, and one she could paint directly without relying on invention. She had with her some books on the work of favorite painters—Van Gogh, Burchfield and Guston. Guston she had met at Yale, Burchfield she knew in the original from several pictures in the collection of the Marion Koogler McNay Art Museum in San Antonio, Van Gogh she had discovered by once buying the largest art book on sale in a local store.

In Miller's family house in Houston hang several large paintings by local talents. They are thickly painted, almost abstract, landscapes. Miller recalls thinking all paintings were thick. One can tell from her early work that she had obviously looked at these pictures, although her efforts were soon to surpass them. Until she moved back to Texas, Miller's powers of observation had not much been used in making her painting; rather, she had been looking at the canvases of her professors and at book reproductions of artists she intuitively admired. As Miller began to consider herself an artist, she found herself compelled to paint by subjects which mattered to her, and by the possibility of pursuing idealistic personal goals. In her first four years as a young painter, Miller painted landscapes which would occasionally include animals.

By 1976, Miller had grown lonely in Flatonia and had also taken a studio in Austin. In 1977, newly married, she had moved to Bee Caves, just outside of Austin. She would keep a studio in Austin until 1984.

The first works in this exhibition are animal portraits dating from 1978, which reflect Miller's deep emotional involvement with animals.

There are approximately a dozen works in this series of paintings on paper. Large in size and scale, they are not quick sketches. Miller took the ideas to the studio ready to realize full-size work. The animals portrayed in *Mean Dog*, 1978, *Cotton and Quails*, 1978, *Big Chicken, Small Dog*, 1978, and *A Chance Meeting*, 1978, are not alone. Each picture and most of the titles are descriptive and usually indicate pairing and confrontation. "Mean" describes the dog who threatens the chicken as another bird looks on. "Cotton" is a dog who strolls by as quails watch. "Big Chicken" is just the size of the "Small Dog" it is paired with, and in *A Chance Meeting*, a rabbit and a chicken are painted in profile—nose to nose. In each work, except the last, the animals portrayed are natural enemies. There seems to be in each case a mutual sizing up or a quizzical curiosity. Yet there is no action, no implied aggression of one beast towards another. *Mean Dog* seems the most threatening and *A Chance Meeting* the most benign. In each case, the animals are painted against a black ground. There is no setting to detract from the detailing, color, brushwork and animation of the subjects.

The paint quality of these works varies quite a bit, which can be explained by the fact that besides using her own observation of animals, Miller was admiring simultaneously the differing styles of Edward Hicks, Henri Rousseau and Courbet, all represented by excellent pictures in the collection of the Dallas Museum of Art. Experimenting with technique, Miller uses broad brush strokes, again painting from Abstract Expressionist training, but there is also skillful drawing with brush, apparent in the expressive animal faces. Great attention has been directed to the fur and feathers. Their natural overall patterning and beautiful textures suggested for the artist new possibilities for paint. Color is applied with a general realism, but liberties are taken when color can indicate mood. For example, the tongue of "Mean Dog" is bright red, and a bold ring of white encircles the eyes of the rabbit in *A Chance Meeting*, indicating ferocity and fear, respectively.

Miller found that the animal portraits were a way of deciding what to paint and they could have an emotional quality as well. Gradually, in 1978 and throughout 1979, Miller began to build up narrative, composing little stories or vignettes which could be played out in the canvases. She made pictures incorporating both the human figure and the landscape, but in general her works were dominated by the presence of animals.

The animals usually outnumber the humans in the paintings, as was the case in Miller's personal surroundings at the ranch. *Cattle with Egrets*, 1979, typical of the paintings of this period, is about three and one-half feet high and is filled with images—figures which overflow off the edges of the canvas, project in from the sides; egrets are shown full face, in profile, in flight and at rest.

These paintings seem to come from personal experience, the titles indicating Miller's inspiration. *Out of the Coop*, 1978, shows chickens escaped from their coop, attracting Miller's three large dogs. No threat is depicted, but the viewer realizes the inevitable outcome. *Crowded Lake*, 1979, shows two human feet dangling into the water from a dock. Lakes are an important part of Miller's landscape. Her painting is a childlike fantasy of a lake crowded with ferocious fish. For Miller noticed that fish, like birds and dogs, have skins which reflect and capture light and change colors as they move. Each fish is abstract and beautiful, and its covering, shape and color are indicative of its role in the animal kingdom.

There are some paintings from 1979, and many from 1980, which openly depict human dramas. *Black Cloud*, 1979, is the first canvas to include a full figure. Miller is trying to paint deep space—different from the space found in abstract painting; one more compatible to narrative. In this painting, she wanted to achieve a complex narrative in a realistic space. The crudely painted figure and the cloud behind it are still stylized; only the woman's hand gestures and the symbolic dark cloud indicate that she is distressed. The most interesting part of the canvas is taken up by the two dogs—one looks directly out at the viewer and the other sniffs the ground, its back to its mistress with no concern for the drama or the audience—it is just being a dog. Miller's composition echoes W.H. Auden's poem *Musée des Beaux Arts*, "Where the dogs go on with their doggy life and the torturer's horse / Scratches its innocent behind on a tree,"[2] telling us that while big human dramas occur, natural events continue on their usual course, little affected by our human problems.

Meeting at Dawn, 1979, *Talking to Eddie,* 1979, and *The Splash*, 1980, follow next. In these paintings, while Miller still continues to explore different ways of separating events on the canvas through different kinds of spatial handling, something else occurs—an ominous figure creeps into the picture. In *Meeting at Dawn*, there is the usual animal confrontation as a coyote creeps across the turkey yard, lurking in a way which might become threatening. Miller has set up a tension between the animals—the coyote is well known to be a natural enemy of the turkey. However, she has also put a wild animal near a sleeping human figure, seen through the window of a house, introducing a more subtle or symbolic element. The coyote is in darkness, the figure in light; one is wild, the other civilized; one wide-awake and predatory, one asleep and vulnerable. Is the shadowy coyote stalking just the turkeys or does he pose a potential threat to the unaware sleeper? Miller says she was not yet very aware of all the possibilities of symbolism.

In *Talking to Eddie*, the artist portrays herself chatting with a neighbor at Flatonia. The animals and insects in the foreground actually are the subjects, rather than the two ordinary figures and the truck in the background. In the middle ground is the real activity of the painting—a hoard of insects, many grasshoppers. The insects are painted in a light patch across the center of the canvas and to the same scale as the birds. Enlarged, they become vaguely threatening. The composition of the canvas reveals Miller's interest in primitive and folk art, both of which are prevalent in Texas collections, galleries and museums, as well as in Persian miniatures, which she saw reproduced in books. From folk painting, she saw how the artist would often make events or objects of lesser importance smaller in scale and put them at the edge or bottom of the canvas. From Persian miniatures, she learned about a method of composition which did not require deep space, but could still separate events or indicate the passage of time. For example, in the famous *A King's Book of Kings* (1520-1530), there is a miniature by Sultan Muhammed which uses a three-tiered composition to indicate the passage of time and which includes the depiction of people in animal pelts (signifying their peaceful coexistence with the animal world). In *Talking to Eddie*, she makes these kind of compositional devices her own. Later, she will use the animal and human dramas in her pictures as well.

Until now, most of Miller's canvases read horizontally. In *The Splash*, Miller uses water to create a diagonal split in the composition—a more advanced and sophisticated device. She paints, in each half, two separate events to equal scale—one human, one animal. At the upper right, a fish jumps in the lake—it is as large as the birds whose attention it catches. At the lower left of the canvas, Miller's family picnics on watermelon. In *Black Cloud*, the animals ignore the human dilemma. In this painting, the animals are seen having a life of their own which Miller paints as equally important to that of the humans. The people in earlier pictures were usually truncated, always small, and in the background. The animals were dominant and up front on the canvas. The people in *The Splash* are unaware of the animal drama—their attention is focused elsewhere. In *The Splash*, while the figures and the animals still do not interact, Miller is realizing the multiplicity of life—that large and small events occur concurrently; that there are different levels of life and experience. She is beginning to question her previous interpretations of life and art.

The Splash also served for Miller as a remembrance of her paternal grandfather who had died four years before. In the picture, he sits with his back to the viewer. The place and the activities depicted are ones Miller associated with him. She recalls, "One of the things which occurs at the ranch is that you can be focused on an activity and outside you'll hear a giant splash and you turn around and there is nothing there." Auden's poem continues:

> In Brueghel's *Icarus*, for instance: how everything turns away
> Quite leisurely from the disaster; the plowman may
> Have heard the splash, the forsaken cry,
> But for him it was not an important failure; the sun shone

In 1979 and 1981, Miller made four important pictures and one drawing based initially upon her desire to experiment with translucence. To experiment technically, she painted a ghost story. *The Ghost of Bride's Camp*, 1979, is based on a tale her grandmother told her in the summers in New Mexico. "Every canyon has one," Miller puts it, describing the traditional tale of the bride killed in an accident on her wedding night. Miller is able to draw freely from the fantasy of family lore largely because her family spends a great deal of time together, much of it in recalling old memories and story telling. For her, this is a normal and logical form of communication, even though events become distorted or exaggerated with retelling over time. She also enjoys the writings of Southern authors J. Frank Dobie and Eudora Welty for much the same qualities.

After she found she had the skill to paint translucent figures, Miller used the technique to paint two canvases, *Dream of a Dolphin Who Was Really My Dog*, 1980, and *The Generous Spirit of Miss Ima*, 1981, as well as the painting on paper, *Miss Ima Visits Diana*, 1981. The last two are tributes to the generous Houston patron of the arts who left her house, Bayou Bend, to the city of Houston as a museum of decorative arts. As a child, Miller recalls Miss Ima Hogg was held up to her and her sisters as having achieved everything that a lady should strive for and as a fine example of a Texas philanthropist. About her upbringing, she says:

> As I grew up in Texas in the 1950s and 1960s, there was a pervasive attitude of state independence and pride. New was better. All things were possible. Houston wasn't going to let the 'old' North tell it how to do things. The generations of Houstonians in my family felt that my siblings and I should adopt this attitude too; so we did. It really wasn't such a bad attitude to grow up with. The energy and self-respect it nurtured has influenced my art. It also affected my decision to stay in Texas, giving me courage to believe that quality art could be produced on one's home turf.[3]

The main subject of the two Miss Ima pictures is somewhat overshadowed by elements which again allow Miller to explore color and surface—each is filled with azalea bushes, lush and in full bloom. In the background of *The Generous Spirit of Miss Ima*, one of the first paintings for which she did extensive research, Miller painted the house at Bayou Bend. She went to the library and read all she could find on the house, the gardens and the lady herself. In the animal paintings which were to follow, Miller would continue to do the same—studying the anatomy, habits and lore of each beast.

Miller uses a dream as the source of *Dream of a Dolphin Who Was Really My Dog*. In the dream, a dolphin is speaking to her: "Touching it, I recognized a personality in it which evolved into my dog." Although the painting falls back on earlier works—using the artist as the character and the same black backgrounds found in the animal portraits—this picture is important because it deals with transformations. Miller was attempting, with white paint, to make transparent figures. This was partly a technical exercise, but it was carried out because transparency suggested to Miller the possibilities of transformation. The dolphin becomes a dog, the dream becomes a reality. Mixing reality and fantasy, drama and daily life, would lead her later to paintings whose subjects were mystical or symbolic change.

Studio Building, 1980, represents an important transition in Miller's work. Since 1976, she had been working in various studios in Austin. Her pictures often recorded city life or events. She was now bored with the tediousness of painting in the urban landscape and using buildings and the human figure. What she found really exciting in this picture were animals, particularly birds. She felt painting the figure had always been a struggle for her—each was different from the next because she could not find a vocabulary for people. Animals, however, she found to be "very consistent as a source for pictures. They are very active and always had my interest." In addition, animals could serve as her strongest metaphor for human emotions, unlike landscape—no matter how expressive.

Smuggling Parrots Across the Border, 1981, is the last picture Miller has made including a human figure. The man in it is the biggest, freshest and most expressionistic figure she ever made. Ironically, he almost disappears behind the basket of birds he carries. The important part of the picture is this large crate bursting full of brightly-colored birds. In this painting, Miller found the animals were enough, and that they could serve her narrative purpose. She now was more interested in rendering animals in paint than the human figure. Skin, fur and feathers offered an endless variety of textures and technical challenges.

Changes in Miller's pictures in the early 1980s were precipitated by some personal factors, as well as aesthetic ones. Four people in Miller's immediate family had been stricken with cancer and a sense of impending doom had settled over her. She felt trapped by waiting for the deaths of the people she loved, and by the realization that adulthood brings with it the loss of the beloved elders of the family. Pictures can be a way of conferring immortality. It now became Miller's concern in her pictures. Miller had always linked her painting to the history of art by her open and deep admiration of great artists. With this new change, Miller tied her work to a tradition which is as old as painting itself—the themes of life and life's forces.

At this point, paradoxically, Miller's paintings ceased to have their usual narrative. Each still had a specific event at the center of its inspiration, but each also incorporated certain homages to art history that became the springboard for its composition. From these two impulses, her own style was beginning to be apparent. Gradually, the paint thickened reflecting her admiration for Soutine, Van Gogh and Guston. The surfaces had a density and a gleam of their own achieved by paint and varnish. Her brushwork began to have its own length and texture. The strokes of paint started to echo the stripes in the animals' fur or the foamy crests atop waves. Color developed anew—she was looking at paintings like *The Icebergs*, 1861, by Frederick Church, newly acquired by the Dallas Museum. She was beginning to sense that color had many sources and that observed color can be used as effectively as that from fantasy.

The paintings from 1981, such as *Undertow, Tempesta,* and *Anticipation*, reflect in their titles Miller's personal and emotional states. She had, until now, invented exchanges between animals based upon common dilemmas—now she was letting fantasy take over with the result that her paintings became both more experimental and more sure. They are boldly new for her in their composition. The subjects demanded a more sophisticated composition and Miller searched her historical vocabulary for new devices.

Using a circular motif as structure, particularly in *Undertow* and *Tempesta,* Miller relies upon devices she had observed in the work of other painters. There is a painting, for example, entitled *The March of Silenus,* 1862, by the American painter William H. Beard (1823-1900), in the collection of the Albright-Knox Art Gallery, which she had seen in reproduction. Beard's subject is a drunken Bacchus, represented as a bear surrounded by goats bearing bunches of grapes. The animals depict man's folly. Miller's 1981 pictures are of more troubled subjects, but like Beard, she also sees animals as vehicles for human frailties and foibles. In order to achieve deep space in his picture, Beard has gathered the action in a circular composition on the canvas, a device which leads the eye finally to the circular patch of blue sky in the distance. There are multiple visual spirals in Miller's painting too. They become a dominant feature in many subsequent works. In *Undertow,* the crab is caught in a circle of color and swirling paint; in *Tempesta,* sheep circle a lake surrounded by dark clouds; and in *Anticipation,* big clouds form a billowing cave around the animals who gaze towards a tornado. Miller is not imagining these events in nature; she is using the Texas landscape—a naturally dramatic one, of tornados, floods and constantly changing sky. She is, however, taking liberties with color and the animals are beginning to be more individual and isolated. *One Rabbit Feeling the Pain of Another,* 1982, for example, is focused on the individual rabbits. Miller has combined the narrative drama of the 1979 and 1980 pictures with the strong focus of the 1978 animal portraits in this painting. It is not as large as *Tempesta* or as tightly composed as *Undertow,* but it is somehow one of her most felt canvases, and signals a change which will develop in 1982 and 1983.

During 1981, Miller made about twelve paintings on paper, continuing to use a circular composition, in a series called *Studies for the Ark.* These studies were not intended for use in a particular painting—they did, however, become the vocabulary for a 1986 picture entitled *The Ark.* The purpose of the drawings was to explore animals in active environments, as well as to express Miller's frustrations about her own world. Each represents a "shorter" idea than found in a painting. With the studies, Miller could try out a lot of animals quickly, as well as experiment with different kinds of composition. These pictures are animals in different atmospheres. They are about pairings, different species together in turmoil. Miller says, "I never could understand all these ark paintings where everything is going so well—all these animals that would kill each other are together—everyone is behaving beautifully." Apparent is a tendency for a coiled or spiralling composition resulting from Miller's admiration of earlier animal painters, in whose pictures the activity often centers around one figure or animal being attacked by a group of others.

In early 1982, Miller made a smaller series of works on paper devoted to dancing bears. The paintings on paper are painted in acrylic, not oil. Because acrylic paint is thinner and because she cannot build up the surface, Miller paints these works on paper quickly. With their immediate

gesture and active brush work, they clearly recall her admiration of
Abstract Expressionism. While the works on paper are not exact studies
for future paintings, Miller feels, "they gave me more freedom to experiment, to be looser and more playful." These pictures are the last in which
Miller can ignore the anatomy of the animals. The form of the animals
now begins to be important to her—the knowledge of their anatomy
paralleling her emotional response to them. The works of George Stubbs
and Sir Edwin Landseer became important to her—she even traveled to
Philadelphia in 1982 to see a survey of Landseer's pictures at the Philadelphia Museum of Art. She now does research (as she did for the Miss
Ima pictures) for each painting and her studio fills with library books and
photographs of bears, leopards, tigers, bighorn sheep, coyotes, ravens
and peacocks.

Miller works on one painting at a time and each takes several months
to complete. To begin a large canvas, she conceives of the subject and
she stretches a canvas to the size she wants. First Miller makes a sketchy
pencil drawing on paper. She transfers this to canvas as an ocher wash.
Next she covers the canvas with thin paint veils to establish a color
scheme. She then begins to paint with large thick strokes. She likes fresh
strokes so she rarely reworks. She aspires to a clear and immediate appearance for the surface. The pictures look deceptively quick because she
does not apply the "final" paint until the undercomposition and color suit
her. The pictures are made by working in long stretches, as many as
twelve hours at a time, then resting, and beginning again.

In 1982, the paintings increased in scale, because, she says, "I needed
more room for composition." At that time, Miller made a conscious decision to begin to explore the variety of life's emotions and to base her paintings on other than fleeing and turbulence. Her paintings begin to be
dense, more complex in both composition and narrative; they say more.
The subjects of her paintings have often been said to be ambiguous, but
for Miller they are still very personal. The 1982 and 1983 paintings seem
even more poignant than those which preceded them. *Leopard Dance,*
1983, for example, is a picture about spiritual transition. Three tigers and
a leopard drape themselves in trees—backs to the viewer. They are four
in number, like the Miller females. They are beautiful, large, full and
sinuous, and they watch a white leopard dance in the distant background, bathed in a brilliant eternal light. The painting has the same circular composition she began to explore in 1981. It pushes the viewer's
eye to the action at the back of the canvas. This picture has the greatest
depth she has achieved thus far. In *Untitled* (Tigers), 1982, three tigers

facing outward watch curiously as monkeys dance. The animals are much closer both to each other and to the surface of the canvas than in *Leopard Dance.* The two paintings taken together are about observation and temptation. They are extremely powerful pictures. Miller painted them on the occasion of her father's death, but for the viewer it isn't important that the personal narrative be obvious, the paintings are strong enough to take over. She says, "I trusted them to transcend somehow."

In 1982, Miller received a cash award from the Dallas Museum which she used to take her first trip to Europe. She went to France, Italy and Spain to visit the great museums—The Louvre, the Uffizi, the Prado—and to see the Old Masters firsthand. She viewed the great battle and hunting scenes and painters such as Delacroix whose *Tiger Hunt*, 1854, and *Lion Devouring a Rabbit*, 1856, are in the collection of The Louvre. In Florence, the work of the 15th-century painter Paolo Uccello was extraordinary inspiration for her because of his method of composing—using dense compositions filled with animals and figures. When she returned to Austin, she had stored up a lot of information.

Another important event was her discovery of the Japanese scrolls of *Chōjū giga* which roughly translates as "frolicking animals." Miller had discovered reproductions of the scrolls just before she went to Europe. The scrolls are attributed to a priest named Tōbā Sōjā Kakuya (1053-1140) and are believed to be his warning of the grave state of moral and spiritual decay of his nation. Animals are shown playing human games and indulging in human vices, yet are portrayed as doing so within the physical limitations of actual animals. There exists in the scrolls an artistic freedom Miller could learn from—a precedent for making animals which play and interact, yet which do not give over into being mere cartoons. In Europe, Miller had found herself looking for ways to paint deep space. *Clowns,* 1983, painted upon her return was her first direct attempt at foreshortening and the use of shadow. Previously, Miller had achieved a sort of space by having the animals looking in a certain direction or by using clouds or trees to form a circle or semicircle around the action, thus focusing the viewer's eye towards the important parts of the canvas. Miller is now able to have both—controlled spatial relationships in her paintings, as well as animals to use as metaphor.

Next come *Swamp* and *Flood*—large canvases, both dated 1983. For Miller, they became important color studies. Each conveys a different mood and exploits animal textures, as well as different natural settings. *Swamp* has calm water as opposed to the rushing water of *Flood,* yet each challenged her technique. One required precise and calculated painting, the other loose, free strokes. She says, "I think there is an ominous

light in both of them—a strange light, a light quality that was super-
natural." Miller had realized in *Leopard Dance* the power of light sources
outside of the canvas and after these two pictures, she uses it often in
later pictures.

In the 1983 pictures, Miller uses exotic animals that are not native to
Texas and landscapes that she doesn't find in her backyard. Moreover,
with more firsthand knowledge, her admiration of many other artists'
work becomes more sophisticated and useful to her. The turbulence of the
1983 pictures gives way to a 1984-1985 series of paintings on canvas and
on paper of animals in moonlight, *Deer Dance,* 1984, and *Leaping Doe,*
1984, which are based upon actual observation, mixed with Miller's
admiration of the work of Tsukioka Yoshitoshi, the 19th-century Japanese
printmaker. Yoshitoshi made a series of woodblock prints entitled *One
Hundred Aspects of the Moon,* using the moon to light his compositions
which often included animals. In Miller's pictures, *Mouthful,* 1984,
Swatting the Moon, 1984, and *Reflection,* 1984, animals relate directly
to the moon and do not just bask in its light—they slap at it, bite it, dive
for it, dance for it, and look into it. In these paintings, the animals' attention is directed to nature rather than to one another. The pictures are
quiet and almost poetic as compared to the previous paintings. The
animals are usually alone and the landscape settings minimal. The moon,
a large part of the composition, again gives Miller's pictures a central
and circular focus.

In another group of small 1985 paintings on canvas and on paper,
including *Moon and Peach,* Miller depicts phases of the moon as it illumi-
nates still lifes of peaches and their leaves. These small and delicate
pictures are filled with two circular forms—one very close up, the other
far away. The ripe and warm peach is distinctly female in its soft, fur-
covered skin. The moon is pockmarked and cool by comparison. The
still life has traditionally been used as a reminder of man's mortality, his
inevitable decay and his transience on earth. The peach will rot, but the
moon will continue to rise in the sky each night. Miller's metaphors are
delicate, almost discreet, in these pictures. If it was the cycle of dying and
death, loss and spiritual awakening which prompted her earlier pictures,
it is the same cycle which occasions these, but Miller has grown calmer
and more deliberate in her art.

Although Miller says this is not intentional, many of the pictures—
particularly those using the moon—can be seen as highly erotic. The moon
appeals to Miller because it transforms itself—constantly changing shape
and color in a natural cycle. It is also a traditional symbol of fertility and

of life's forces. Miller gives more attention to some natural phenomena over others, like the rushing water often found in her pictures, especially where she can learn from it technically; however, usually these subjects are ones with powerful sexual associations in literature and art.

On a second trip to Europe in the summer of 1984, Miller saw De Chirico's late still lifes and admired his method of composing objects close to the front of the canvas. Using this technique and moonlight as a subject, but with emphasis on it as a source of color, she continued in a *Nighteaters* series painted between 1984 and 1985. Some are still lifes, some are of animals and their prey. They are certainly the most skillful pictures Miller has painted to date. Each canvas is small, the same size as her works on paper. The series is done on both surfaces, as a challenge in scale to the previous large works and as a challenge of brushwork in acrylics and oils. She succeeds in making complete, technically astonishing pictures which seem almost to belong to another time.

As she often does, Miller varies her pictures in sequence: one is about night, the next daylight; one is very tightly structured, the next loosely painted. Because *Nighteaters* were so dark and controlled, *Salmon Run* and *Bathing Tigers,* both 1984, are bright sparkling pictures. The compositions are vertical rather than horizontal, and they are both painted with very small brushstrokes—"dots and pricks and dabs" of paint represent the water. "Water," she says, "is like ghosts in technical handling." She uses great expressionism to advantage here.

Aesop's Crow, 1985, is also painted in small quick motions. The detail of the birds' feathers is the main source of interest and the element which unites the canvas. The light hits the crows and the peacocks, reflecting off of them in colors. The picture has a definite clarity. "I think the fact that I put peacocks in [the picture] dictated that I give the other birds the same detail their feathers deserved. To make the composition united, I had to use that small brushstroke on the other birds." Miller, who has read the fables, painted the picture as much for its moral as for its historical references. Crows are symbolically used in both Japanese (symbolic of the sun) and Chinese (symbolizing filial piety) painting. She had for a long time been thinking of making a painting of a grouping of birds because she kept coming across this composition in the history of animal genre painting which she admired. She tried, she says, to focus on the bird being attacked, but the final composition, "exploded more than it focused." This accident of composition gave Miller what she had felt at other times she could not achieve—pictorial space which has foreground, middle and background. The picture is light and much more complex than any which precede it. It also has moral, as well as personal references—this time Miller will not reveal which bird is herself and which others represent her family and friends, although it is apparent the picture tells an intimate story.

Zebras and Hyenas, 1985, is one of a very few of Miller's pictures in which animals are actually attacked by other animals. It recalls Landseer and his Flemish predecessors Paul de Vos, Franz Snyders and Rubens, in whose works dogs lunge at stags and bears at wolves and foxes. It is fascinating that Miller's style came to her early and was fully developed before she knew these works. Her canvases were large and dramatically intense from the start. However, as she develops she uses historical precedent to confirm the direction of her work, rather than as a direct influence on each painting.[4]

Doing research for *Zebras and Hyenas,* Miller read conflicting accounts of the zebra pack's behavior during an attack. One report claimed the animals fled as a group, the adult pack protecting the infants at the center. The other research claimed the animals broke apart in order that the enemy would be confused by the breaking stripes. From the latter, Miller realized a similar arrangement could be achieved by substituting brush strokes for stripes.

The next works are a series of paintings on paper, and all are dated 1985. They represent animals masquerading as other animals. They are titled *Raven as Peacock, Rabbit Parading as a Fox,* and *Wolf Dancing as a Deer.* The sources for these are multiple. The winter ceremonial dances of the Taos Pueblo Indians in New Mexico is an important one. On this occasion, the Indians put on the skins of animals they hunt in order to call the spirits of new animals. Other sources are again historical—Japanese prints in which animals represent changelings and become humans, Greek mythology, and the parables in the Bible in which animals have strength or weakness, prophetic, magical or spiritual properties.

Recently, Miller has made six paintings on paper of animal spirits and demons. Depicted are animals with their own ghosts and demon skeletons. The deer in *Deer Spirit,* 1986, seems to call forth its own spirit, while in *Confronting Demons,* 1986, the subjects—a monkey and its ghostlike skeleton—are menacingly face to face, backed by a full, red moon. These pictures call upon the tradition of ghost and demon images found in the Japanese prints of Utagawa Kuniyoshi (1797-1861) and his pupil Yoshitoshi. Based upon folk tales which form the basis for teaching Japanese religions, the spirit images are appealing to Miller in the same way as the stories and Texas and New Mexico lore she heard from her family. Tales are exaggerated and fantastic, and they depend for their impact upon the settling of good over evil. *Confronting Demons,* 1986, takes its composition from a Kuniyoshi print, *Ghost Skeleton* (n.d.), in which a huge skeleton looms into the picture frame from a corner. The pictures move from the technical proficiency found in Miller's still lifes into more abstract possibilities. They provide an occasion to return to painted translucence and to use a new stroke—a gesture which is almost calligraphic. They use animals in confrontation as did the animal portraits of 1978; they use the moonlight discovered in 1983, all to new advantage. The composition need not be as structured as that of *Zebras and Hyenas.* The demons and the spirits are vehicles to make compositions which do not rely on traditional structure. The animals acquire human gestures and enter our world; they become personified by using human gestures, yet they become mysterious and transformed. In *Exhale,* 1986, from the open mouth of the bear come multiple bear skeletons and bear ghosts and bear demons. The live bear confronts its own history and prehistory.

Into the centuries of animal paintings, one tries to place Miller's works. She clearly does not hesitate to copy, admire, pay homage to, or be inspired by her predecessors. From the centuries of animal paintings, one attempts to find those which match Miller's creatures. Miller explains:

> In Japanese prints the Japanese tend to animate so many things—a tea kettle can become a badger and people can anthropomorphize into animals, but that's not the way Aesop uses them. He uses them as metaphor. Both are possibilities to me. I like those choices. They seem to be missing for me in a lot of art today.

The inevitable interaction between humans and animals creates endless possibilities for depiction. We humans are curious about these near-to-human beings. Their ability to coexist peacefully on the earth, as well as their natural animosities, allow Miller to reflect upon them as examples of ourselves. They are strong, instinctual, adept at survival; yet, they can also be weak. They are curious and can be clever or stupid. They cannot be observed without obstacle, for they have camouflage behind which they can hide their characters. They are perhaps us, without conditioning, our emotions untrained and unleashed, and they provide unarguable examples of all our ways and moods. They can be used to illustrate what we cannot observe in ourselves. Animals have their own world and standards of measure. They face wind, rain and natural enemies. We have acid rain, nuclear disaster and crime. The world we humans inhabit is as harsh in its own way as nature is to animals. Miller understands both worlds as connected. She sees, "life as dependent on life."

Although her paintings draw freely from the past, they are never self-conscious. Few artists today have the means to express human emotions, nor has it been acceptably modern to make art which draws upon the dramas of pride and suffering. Because Miller's paintings do, her works must be viewed from a large perspective. They are important artistically—her technique, color and composition are extremely accomplished. They can also be appreciated from a private viewpoint, in that each represents an event which touches us—touches humanity, strong or weak, silly or sober, nurturers or destroyers of life. Miller believes in the preservation of both life and humanity. She wants for her art a clarity which filters out trivia and focuses on the larger issues. Thus far, hers has been a most successful philosophy.

Notes

[1] All artist's statements are taken from conversations between the artist and the author, 1980-1986.

[2] Auden, W.H., *A Little Treasury of Modern Poetry* (New York: Charles Scribners Sons, 1952), pp. 454, 455. I am indebted to Cheryl Blissitte and Polly Morrice for bringing this to my attention.

[3] Artist's statement in Barbara Rose and Susie Kalil, *Fresh Paint: The Houston School* (Houston: The Museum of Fine Arts, 1985), p. 154.

[4] It is also worth noting that I can find only two other women who painted animal pictures on a heroic scale, English painter Lady Elizabeth Butler (1850?-1933) and the Frenchwoman Rosa Bonheur (1822-1899).

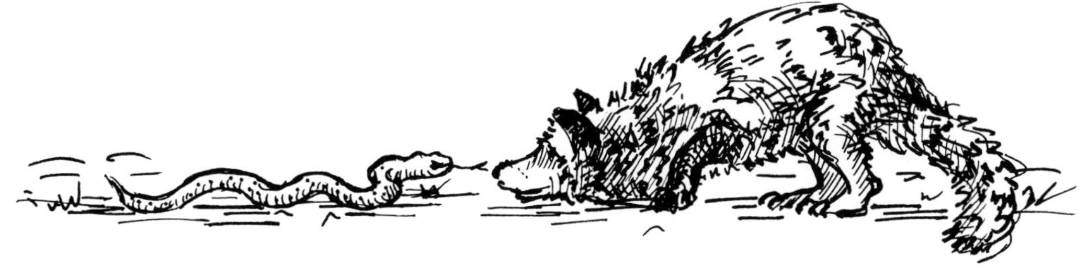

Melissa Miller:
A Wondrous World of Animals
Douglas G. Schultz

In her relatively brief yet exceptionally productive career, Melissa Miller has been searching continuously for her own artistic "vocabulary." She readily acknowledges that, in terms of content and technique, she draws upon a wide variety of art-historical sources; in this regard, she follows the tradition of learning from earlier masters as she experiments with various compositional devices as well as with different approaches to the rendering of surfaces and explores the ways in which a range of emotions might be conveyed through choices of different subject matter. Inspired both psychologically and artistically by numerous painters throughout the history of art, Miller has stated that specific references can be made to her particular interests at the time she was painting a distinct picture. Indeed, the playful nature of her animal characters is reminiscent of a gamut of cultures and artistic endeavors as diverse as ancient Japanese scrolls and animated cartoons of the 20th century. Her dynamic compositions and concern for meticulously rendered detail recall as well the abundant still lifes and energetic animal paintings typical of the northern Baroque tradition. Miller's use of vibrant colors brings to mind those seen in animated films as well as the vivid hues of many Abstract Expressionist works; drawn too from Abstract Expressionism is Miller's emphasis on the picture's surface filled with vigorous brushwork.[1]

Recalling various early encounters with art, Miller has commented:

> For my birthday, when I was about eight, I asked for and received a book entitled *An Introduction to Great Masterpieces of Painting.* I spent a lot of time looking at it, and oddly enough, it's those reproductions which stand out as my first encounter with painting. When I was nineteen, I went to The Museum of Modern Art, New York. I walked into the room of Monet's large *Water Lilies* paintings and for the first time felt I knew what painting could be about. For years now, I have kept four books in close proximity when I paint: a book of Van Gogh, a catalogue of Guston's late works, a book of Japanese art, and a book on Burchfield. Whenever I need energy or stimulation I peruse one of these, because even in reproduction, most of the works seem to me to be living organisms.[2]

Such a statement makes evident her love for painting and her genuine and deep-rooted enthusiasm for diverse art historical sources and their potential for inspiration.

As an art student in college from 1969 to 1974, Miller had been trained in the aesthetics of Abstract Expressionism with its emphasis on brushstrokes as form and content and the importance of color and surface. Such concerns continue to be evident in her paintings. A work such as *Smuggling Parrots Across the Border,* 1981, with its lush color, loaded brushwork and patterning of surface, reflects her academic training as well as her interest—developed during the 1970s—in depicting narrative. Miller had begun by painting what was familiar to her—an observed occurrence on her family's ranch in the Southwest or a known specific incident or cultural phenomenon. She became increasingly interested in the wild and domesticated animals on the ranch and subconsciously began to use them as subjects, creating lurking, threatening presences which, for her, were symbolic of the darker side of life and which reflected personal anxieties and family tragedies that she had been experiencing.

During the formative years following her graduation from college, Miller was inspired by the regionalist attitudes of Thomas Hart Benton and the Canadian artist, Emily Carr (1871-1945). She found appealing their identification with their own origins. In her work Miller sought to emulate their psychologically charged, symbolic depictions of man and his environs; however, she struggled with rendering the human figure and found herself rejecting it in favor of animals and birds, subjects that she found to be exciting and active and that held her interest.

With paintings such as *Tempesta* and *Anticipation,* both from 1981, her works became bigger and bolder with the animals carrying the narrative; the subjects gave her the opportunity as well to develop her lush painterly technique in the rendering of the various textures of fur, feathers and dramatic skies. In reflecting back on that period in her life, the artist sees these paintings, with their sense of doom in the depictions of the sinister forces of nature—the approaching storm or tornado—as analogies to events surrounding her life. However, the paintings transcend these metaphors for personal experience and continue to become more important in pictorial terms because of the ambiguity of meaning and innumerable ways of interpretation.

The artist's first trip to Europe in 1982 deeply affected her art; there she was exposed to a wealth of artistic sources and aesthetic possibilities, ranging from the works of the Italian Renaissance to Dutch and Flemish Baroque still lifes to 19th-century French Romantic paintings to Oriental scrolls. In conversation, Miller has recalled her discovery of and fascination with Japanese paintings of frolicking animals—the handscrolls in the narrative or *E-Maki* style from the late-12th century—in which rabbits or mice, for example, engage in certain human activities but only within the context of the physical limitations of their particular anatomy.

The narrative seems possible yet absurd, which is one way of describing the actions of the participants in *Leopard Dance,* 1983, or *Clowns,* 1983, with its playful monkeys and rabbits dancing on stilts.

After her visit to Europe, Miller's painterly compositions became more complex and the results were often large canvases filled with intricate and involved formalistic elements which added to the drama and movement of the works. She cites Paolo Uccello's use of foreshortened fallen lances to structure the pictorial space in *The Battle of San Romano,* c. 1455,[3] as being particularly instructive in helping her to depict deeper space in her compositions. More obvious sources might be the swirling Baroque composition of Rubens' *The Lion Hunt,* 1615-18,[4] and works by such 19th-century French painters as Delacroix and Géricault, both of whom depicted powerful yet graceful animals. In the arrangement of pictorial elements in such works as *Leopard Dance* and *Flood,* both of 1983, the influence of Delacroix's works, with their circular, tempestuous compositions, and Géricault, who presented the actions of his subjects in the foreground, may be seen.

Miller is not a serious student of art history but rather is a painter who is young and enthusiastic about the act of painting. She loves having friends and acquaintances share with her reproductions and illustrations of art works involving animal imagery, or discovering on her own the work of old masters. Her painting *Aesop's Crow,* 1985, is an excellent example. The inspiration is a work with which she is familiar, in the collection of the Sarah Campbell Blaffer Foundation in Houston, entitled *The Crow Exposed* by the 17th-century Dutch painter Melchior d'Hondecoeter[5] . Although Miller depicts a variety of birds common and indigenous to North America—the cardinal, meadowlark, mallard duck, pheasant, turkey, quail and even the peacock—in comparison to the strange and exotic species that d'Hondecoeter portrayed, she is illustrating the same fable, *The Vain Jackdaw* by Aesop.

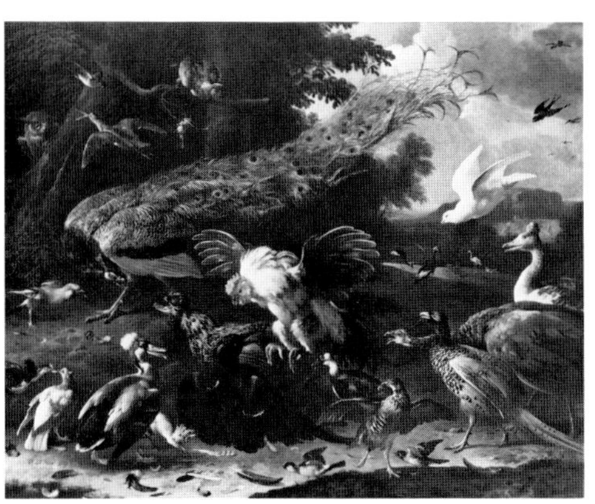

Melchior d'Hoedercoeter
The Crow Exposed, c. 1680
oil on canvas
67 x 83¼"
Collection Sarah Campbell Blaffer Foundation, Houston, Texas

The god Jupiter determined, it is said, to select a king over the birds, and made a proclamation that, on a certain day, all the birds should present themselves to him when he would choose the most beautiful among them to be king. The jackdaw, knowing his own plainness, searched through the woods and fields and collected the feathers that had fallen from the wings of other birds. Then he stuck them all over his body, hoping by this trick to make himself the most beautiful of all. When the appointed day arrived and the birds assembled before Jupiter, the jackdaw made his appearance in his many-feathered finery. On seeing his fine plumage Jupiter proposed to make him king, but the rest of the birds indignantly protested at this, and each plucked from him his own feathers, until the jackdaw was once more nothing but a plain jackdaw. *Fine feathers don't make fine birds.*[6]

The theme of this work offered Miller an opportunity to indulge her interest in depicting the lush, often iridescent plumage of her subjects, to enjoy the fantasy of animal transformation and to realize the possibility of using the animal metaphor to illustrate man's common and moral dilemmas and shared experiences.

She is comfortable with the satirical and humorous nature of her work. It is within these contexts that Miller has expressed her admiration for William Beard, the 19th-century American painter who used animals to satirize human folly and error, and the Victorian painter Sir Edwin Landseer, whose depictions of anthropomorphized or majestic animals were either comments on human behavior or inspirational analogies for human virtues.

Miller is aware of the different cultural traditions that used the fantasy of transformed animals. A variation on this genre is her depiction of animals transformed into other animals through various disguises; this was the subject of her 1985 series of works on paper inspired by an Indian deer dance—an actual dramatization of myth and ritual in which the spirits of the hunter and the hunted are the protagonists—which she has seen during her many visits to New Mexico. These experiences reinforced her belief in regionalism as an artistic source of inspiration. Works from this series, such as *Owl in Sheep's Clothing, Rabbit Parading as a Fox* or *Baboon in Leopard Cape* are overtly fantastical and at the same time reminiscent of her earlier work like *Untitled* (Tigers), 1982, or *Territory,* 1983, which conveyed the same sense of angst and uneasiness. The contrast between the light-hearted and the sinister is even more ironic in these works because the animals are in the guise of their natural enemies.

Another group of works on paper, from 1984-85, is referred to as the *Nighteaters* series. Works from this series, such as *Nighteaters: Corn,* 1984, and *Nighteaters: Shoreline,* 1985, attest to Miller's love of painting, her consummate skill as a painter and her mastery of traditional compositions and themes as seen in the art historical precedents of 17th-century Flemish still life painters such as Jan Fyt and Franz Snyders, whose work she enjoys so much. Miller, inspired by reproductions of these artists' paintings, created vignette-like compositions which are reminiscent of

Snyders, whose still lifes are filled with various fish and game, and fruits and vegetables spilling off tabletops; they also relate to Fyt's depiction of farmyard fowl or a kennel and his still lifes which are activated by monkeys, dogs or live fish. In contrast to the examples by Fyt and Snyders, Miller's paintings are more fanciful, more surreal, and certainly more foreboding because of their nocturnal settings; however, like those artists she admires, she too is involved with depicting still lifes enlivened by animate creatures, and finds exciting the myriad possibilities that these combinations offer.

Never limiting herself to one particular source of inspiration, Miller refers to the still lifes of Giorgio de Chirico for the *Nighteaters* series. While visiting the Venice Biennale in 1984 as a participating artist, she saw and was taken by DeChirico's paintings exhibited there. She was intrigued by his placement of large, dense still lifes so close to the foreground, set against insignificant landscapes; this arrangement was referred to specifically in her own *Nighteaters: Raccoon and Cabbage* of 1984.

Miller is ever conscious of the innumerable sources of visual stimulation available to her but uses them primarily as a means to her own personal and aesthetic ends and to her own particular set of goals and priorities. For example, in *Salmon Run,* a major painting done in 1984, she describes survival and the balancing forces of nature forcefully and vividly. There is no peaceable kingdom or fantasy here. Miller once again establishes a framework for her composition based upon such sources as turbulent Baroque paintings or Oriental scrolls and prints which often portray cascading waters; she is clearly interested here in the play of light on water as well as the consideration of different kinds of brushstrokes—drips and drabs, dots and splatters—and how the paint can interact on the painting's surface. Such interests clearly reflect her art school training in the Abstract Expressionist style.

Miller works on only one painting at a time. While she immerses herself completely in her current project, with its specific and immediate goals, she is always conscious of her own aesthetic history. Her latest work, *The Ark,* 1986, culminates various concerns of the artist which date back to 1981 when she completed an extensive series of small paintings on paper entitled *Studies for the Ark.* This group depicts pairs of animals caught in precarious natural predicaments, often swirling, rising waters. In such ways, this painting relates to *Anticipation,* 1981, in its portrayal of threatening natural forces, and possibly, in its use of animal relationships as metaphors for human ones. Here Miller relies on the Old Testament story of Noah's Ark for her imagery. She conveys as well the traditional theme derived from the story which teaches the importance of man's and animal's coexistence with nature and with each other. Miller has pointed out that this painting is about relationships but is quick to admit that she is depicting a "not so peaceful kingdom." The irony here is that Miller does not include the ark in the painting; thus, an ambiguity is created, which is totally in keeping with Miller's intentions.

Miller's paintings show a consistency in theme and execution. Of the influence of centuries of painters and paintings, she said, "One of my greatest joys is looking at artists' work. I still take things from other artists but the context is my own. I trust my own mind in doing these paintings. The way I do this is unique."[7]

In her work of the last nine years, and especially in *The Ark,* Miller has found her own artistic vocabulary through her assimilation of traditional imagery and conventional painterly technique; in the end, what she has created is a wondrous world of animals that reflects her view of life and nature, one which has universal appeal.

Notes

[1] All artist's statements and quotations are taken from a taped interview of the artist by Linda L. Cathcart, Houston, March 14, 1986, as well as numerous telephone conversations with the artist, April 1986.

[2] Artist's statement in Barbara Rose and Susie Kalil, *Fresh Paint: The Houston School* (Houston: The Museum of Fine Arts, 1985), p. 154.

[3] Collection National Gallery, London.

[4] Collection Alte Pina Kothek, Munich.

[5] I am indebted to Richard Mühlberger, Director of the Museum of Fine Arts, Springfield, Massachusetts, for kindly bringing this to my attention.

[6] Aesop, *The Book of Fables* (New York and London: Frederick Warne & Co., Inc., 1963), p. 14.

[7] Charles Kaufman, "Portrait of a Hill Country Artist," *Austin American-Statesman* (Austin), Onward magazine section, Oct. 1, 1985, p. 16.

Dimensions are given in inches,
height preceding width.

A Chance Meeting, 1978
alkyd and acrylic on paper
22 x 28″
Collection Dr. and Mrs. Earl Koile

Big Chicken, Small Dog, 1978
alkyd and acrylic on paper
22 x 28″
Collection Mr. and Mrs. R.B. Bowen

Cotton and Quails, 1978
alkyd and acrylic on paper
22 x 28″
Collection Mrs. Vernon L. Miller

Mean Dog, 1978
alkyd and acrylic on paper
22 x 28″
Collection Dr. M. Marjorie Menefee

Out of the Coop, 1978
oil on canvas
36 x 50″
Collection the artist

Cattle with Egrets, 1979
oil on canvas
42 x 34″
Collection Dr. Mary Lovey Wood, Austin, Texas

Crowded Lake, 1979
oil on canvas
50 x 44″
Collection Mrs. Vernon L. Miller

Meeting at Dawn, 1979
oil on canvas
40 x 50″
Collection Dr. M. Marjorie Menefee

Talking to Eddie, 1979
oil on canvas
48 x 40″
Collection Basil N. Scaljon and
F. Lynne Wilkerson, San Antonio

The Black Cloud, 1979
oil on canvas
30 x 36″
Collection the artist

The Ghost of Bride's Camp, 1979
oil on canvas
28 x 38″
Collection the artist

Dream of a Dolphin Who Was Really My Dog, 198
oil on canvas
30 x 38″
Collection the artist

Studio Building, 1980
oil on canvas
52 x 44″
Collection Mr. and Mrs. William H.H. Rees

The Splash, 1980
oil on canvas
40 x 60″
Collection Wayland and Ruth Brill

Anticipation, 1981
oil on canvas
50 x 80″
Collection Mrs. Vernon L. Miller

Miss Ima Visits Diana, 1981
acrylic on paper
23 x 29″
Collection AMOCO Production Company

Smuggling Parrots Across the Border, 1981
oil on canvas
42 x 50″
Collection Malou Flato and John Taliaferro

Studies for the Ark: Alligators, 1981
acrylic on paper
23 x 29″
Collection Polly Little and Mark Lavatelli

Studies for the Ark: Bird Against the Wind, 1981
acrylic on paper
23 x 29″
Collection Bill and Janet Kennedy, Austin

Studies for the Ark: Black Swans, 1981
acrylic on paper
23 x 29″
Collection Mr. and Mrs. Edward Spevack,
Huntington, New York

Studies for the Ark: Coyotes and Roadrunners, 1981
acrylic on paper
23 x 29″
Private Collection, Dallas

Studies for the Ark: Ducks, 1981
acrylic on paper
23 x 29″
Collection Dr. M. Marjorie Menefee

Studies for the Ark: Eye of the Storm, 1981
acrylic on paper
24 x 30″
Collection Sherry L. Bryan

Studies for the Ark: Snakes, 1981
acrylic on paper
23 x 29″
Collection Atlantic Richfield Company,
Corporate Art Collection

Tempesta, 1981
oil on canvas
54 x 62″
Collection Mr. and Mrs. Oliver R. Mattingly

The Generous Spirit of Miss Ima, 1981
oil on canvas
50 x 60″
Collection the artist

Undertow, 1981
oil on linen
38 x 42½″
Collection Dr. and Mrs. Earl Koile

Bear Dance in Canyon, 1982
acrylic on paper
23 x 29″
Collection Dr. and Mrs. Stephen A. Szygenda

Bear Dance in Clearing, 1982
acrylic on paper
22 x 28″
Collection Atlantic Richfield Company,
Corporate Art Collection

Bear Dance in River, 1982
acrylic on paper
23 x 29″
Private Collection, Houston

Fox Dance at Dusk, 1982
acrylic on paper
23 x 29″
Bob Butler and Sonny Burt, Dallas

One Rabbit Feeling the Pain of Another, 1982
oil on linen
50 x 42″
Collection Betty Moody and Bill Steffy

Pack and Possums, 1982
oil on canvas
54 x 64″
Collection Mr. and Mrs. Roy S. O'Connor, Houston

Untitled (Tigers), 1982
oil on canvas
58 x 70″
Collection Bob Wilson

Clowns, 1983
oil on linen
56 x 76″
Collection Mr. and Mrs. I.H. Kempner III

Conversation on Stilts, 1983
acrylic on paper
30 x 22″
Collection The First National Bank of Chicago

Flood, 1983
oil on linen
59 x 95″
Collection The Museum of Fine Arts, Houston:
Museum purchase with funds from
Texas Eastern Corporation

Ice Cave, 1983
acrylic on paper
23 x 29″
Collection Anne S. Dayton

Leopard Dance, 1983
oil on linen
60 x 80″
Private Collection, Houston

Moon, 1983
acrylic on paper
29 x 23″
Collection Paul F. Walter

Orange Bear, 1983
acrylic on paper
30 x 22″
Collection Ms. Kenny Griffith Baldwin,
Houston, Texas

Stork Shadow, 1983
acrylic on paper
30 x 22″
Collection Mr. and Mrs. A.L. Ballard

Swamp, 1983
oil on linen
72 x 59″
Collection Holly Solomon, New York

Swatting the Moon, 1983
acrylic on paper
29 x 22″
Collection Mr. and Mrs. Roy S. O'Connor,
Houston

Territory, 1983
oil on linen
69 x 116″
Collection PaineWebber Group Inc.

Bathing Tiger, 1984
acrylic on paper
30 x 22″
Collection John and Susie Kalil

Deer Dance, 1984
oil on linen
84 x 67″
Private Collection, New York
Courtesy Holly Solomon Gallery

Leaping Doe, 1984
acrylic on paper
30 x 22″
Collection The First National Bank of Chicago

Moon and Peach, 1984
oil on linen
18 x 20″
Collection Mr. and Mrs. Ben F. Love, Houston

Mouthful, 1984
acrylic on paper
22 x 30″
Collection Mr. and Mrs. Martin Gutner

Nighteaters: Corn, 1984
acrylic on paper
22 x 30″
Collection Mr. and Mrs. Alfred H. Ebert, Houston

Nighteaters: Raccoon and Cabbage, 1984
oil on linen
24 x 34″
Courtesy Texas Gallery, Houston

Piggyback, 1984
acrylic on paper
30 x 22″
Collection Mr. and Mrs. Marvin Gerstin

Reflection, 1984
acrylic on paper
29 x 23″
Collection Mrs. Phyllis Teplitz

Salmon Run, 1984
oil on linen
90 x 60″
Collection Thomas and Shirley Davis

Secret, 1984
acrylic on paper
22 x 30″
Collection Don Blaustein

Aesop's Crow, 1985
oil on linen
66 x 72″
Promised Gift of Mr. and Mrs. Armand J. Castellani
to the Collection of the Albright-Knox Art Gallery,
Buffalo, New York

Baboon in Leopard Cape, 1985
acrylic on paper
23 x 29″
Collection Laila and Thurston Twigg-Smith

Bobcat with Falconhead, 1985
acrylic on paper
23 x 29″
Collection Mike Chesser, Los Angeles

Lioness in Zebra Skin, 1985
acrylic on paper
22 x 30″
Collection Robin and Alexander Stuart

Moon Trio, 1985
oil on linen
18 x 20″
Collection Carol A. Straus

Nighteaters: Owl, 1985
oil on linen
24 x 34″
Collection the artist

Nighteaters: Shoreline, 1985
acrylic on paper
23 x 29″
Private Collection, New York
Courtesy Holly Solomon Gallery

Owl in Sheep's Clothing, 1985
acrylic on paper
22 x 30″
Collection Mr. and Mrs. Sanford W. Criner Jr.

Rabbit Parading as a Fox, 1985
acrylic on paper
29 x 23″
Collection Thomas H. and Suzanne B. Dungan

Raven as Peacock, 1985
acrylic on paper
30 x 22″
Collection Loretta and Robert K. Lifton

Seventh Day Moon, 1985
oil on linen
18 x 20″
Private Collection

Wolf Dancing as Deer, 1985
acrylic on paper
29 x 23″
Collection Mr. and Mrs. S. Patrick Woodson III

Zebras and Hyenas, 1985
oil on linen
72 x 84″
Collection Archer M. Huntington Art Gallery,
The University of Texas at Austin,
Michener Collection Acquisition Fund, 1986

Confronting Demons, 1986
acrylic on paper
22 x 30″
Private Collection, Houston

Deer Spirit, 1986
acrylic on paper
29 x 23″
Collection Mr. and Mrs. Edward R. Hudson Jr.

Exhale, 1986
acrylic on paper
23 x 29″
Private Collection

Flight from Demons, 1986
acrylic on paper
29 x 23″
Courtesy Texas Gallery, Houston

Smoky Spirits, 1986
acrylic on paper
29 x 23″
Collection Mr. and Mrs. Fred M. Halpern

The Ark, 1986
oil on linen
Two panels, each 67 x 84″
Courtesy Texas Gallery and Holly Solomon Gallery
(not illustrated)

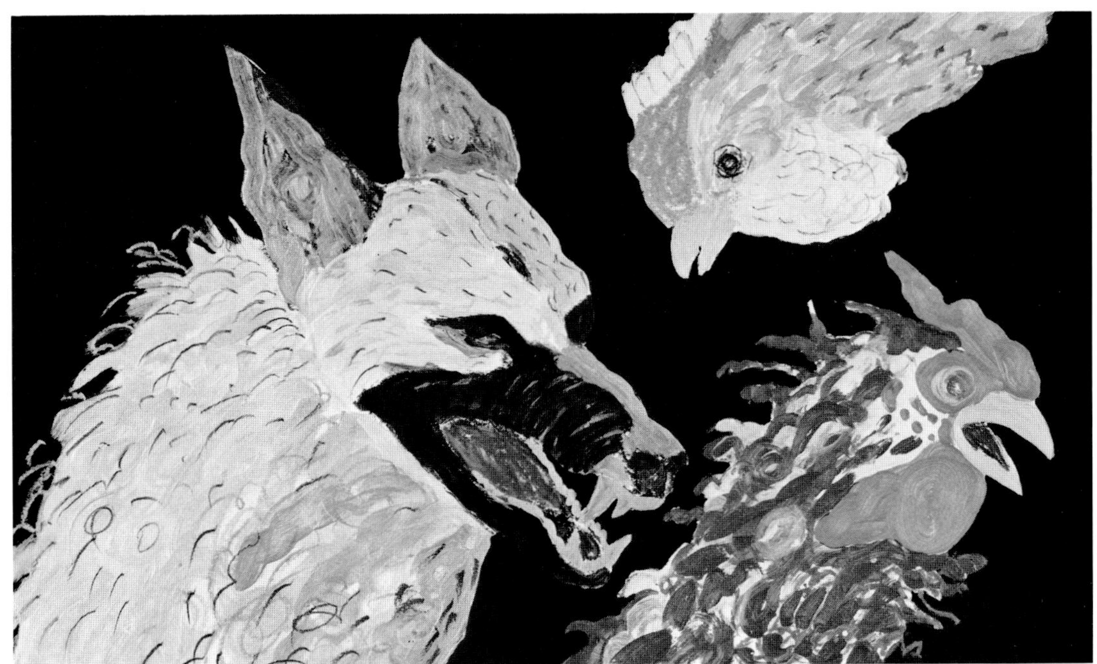

Mean Dog, 1978
alkyd and acrylic on paper
22 x 28″
Collection Dr. M. Marjorie Menefee

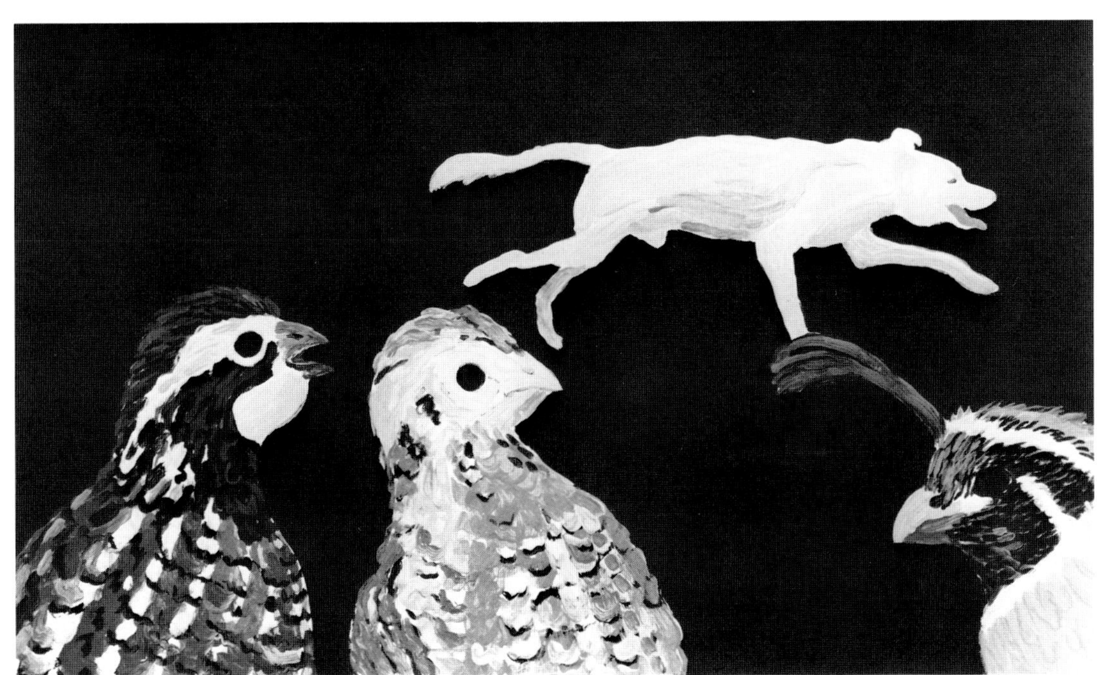

Cotton and Quails, 1978
alkyd and acrylic on paper
22 x 28″
Collection Mrs. Vernon L. Miller

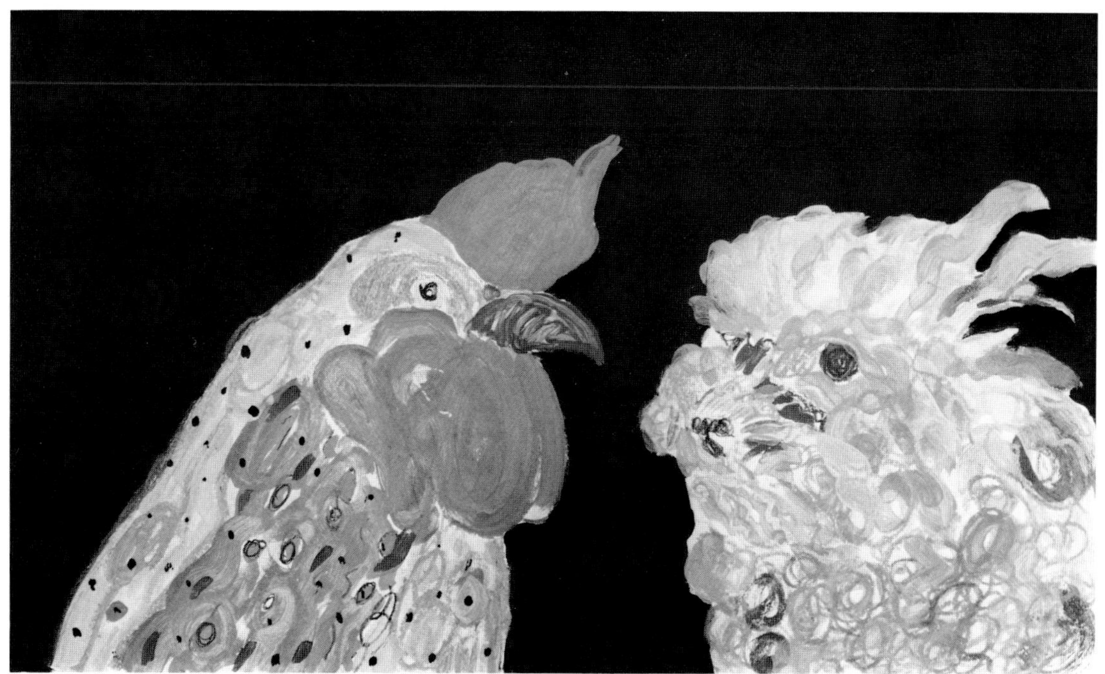

Big Chicken, Small Dog, 1978
alkyd and acrylic on paper
22 x 28″
Collection Mr. and Mrs. R.B. Bowen

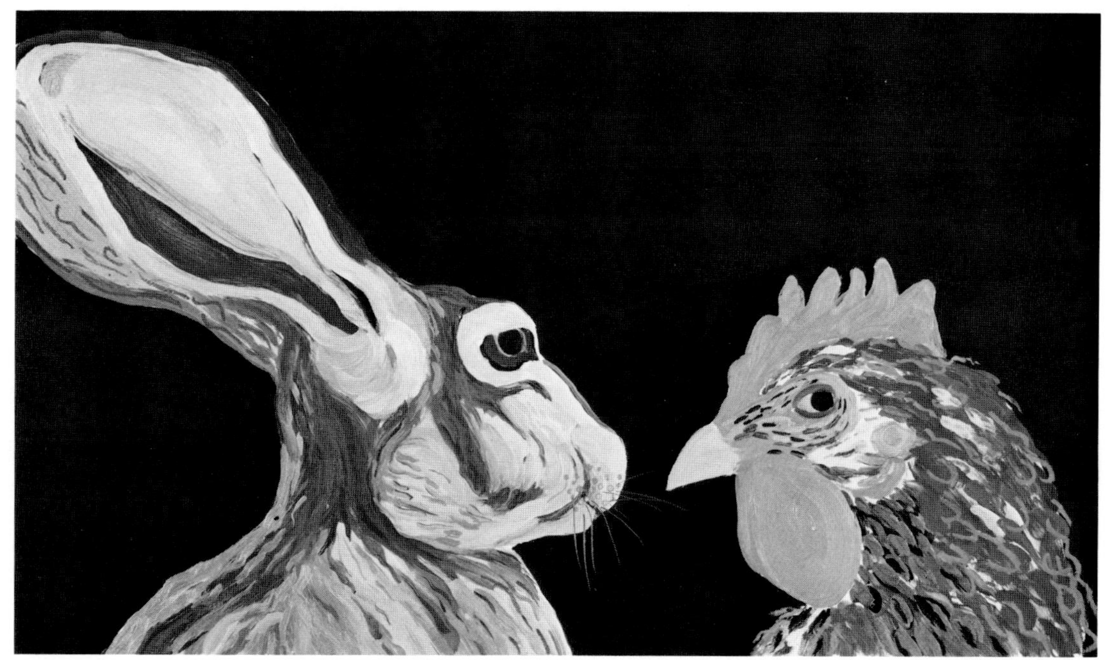

A Chance Meeting, 1978
alkyd and acrylic on paper
22 x 28″
Collection Dr. and Mrs. Earl Koile

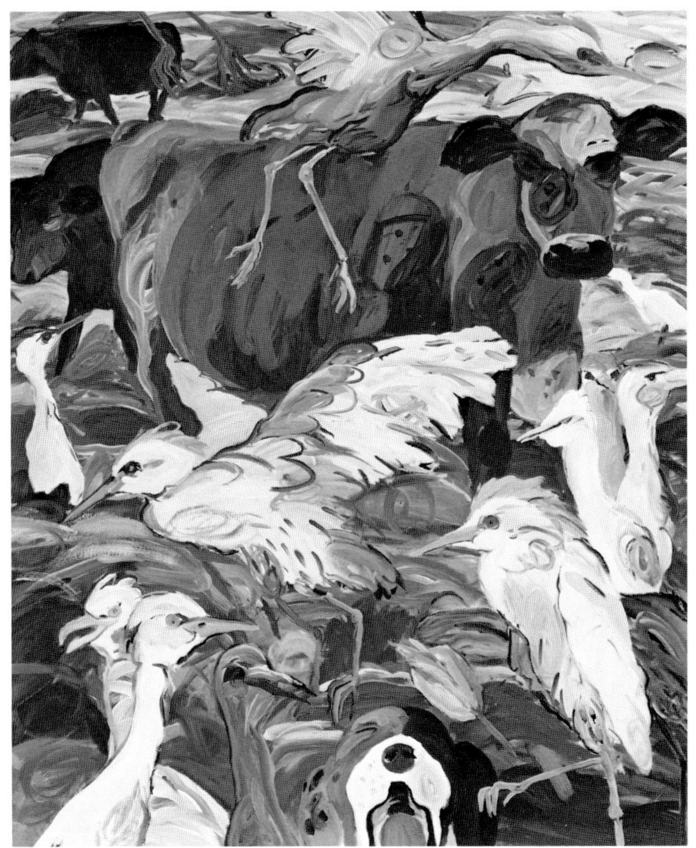

Cattle with Egrets, 1979
oil on canvas
42 x 34″
Collection Dr. Mary Lovey Wood, Austin, Texas

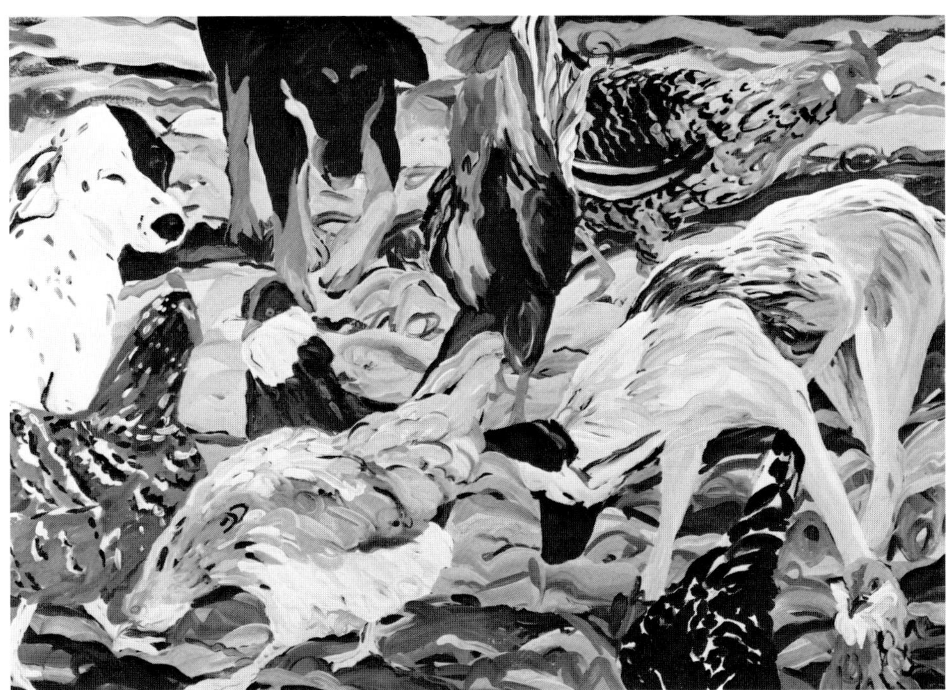

Out of the Coop, 1978
oil on canvas
36 x 50″
Collection the artist

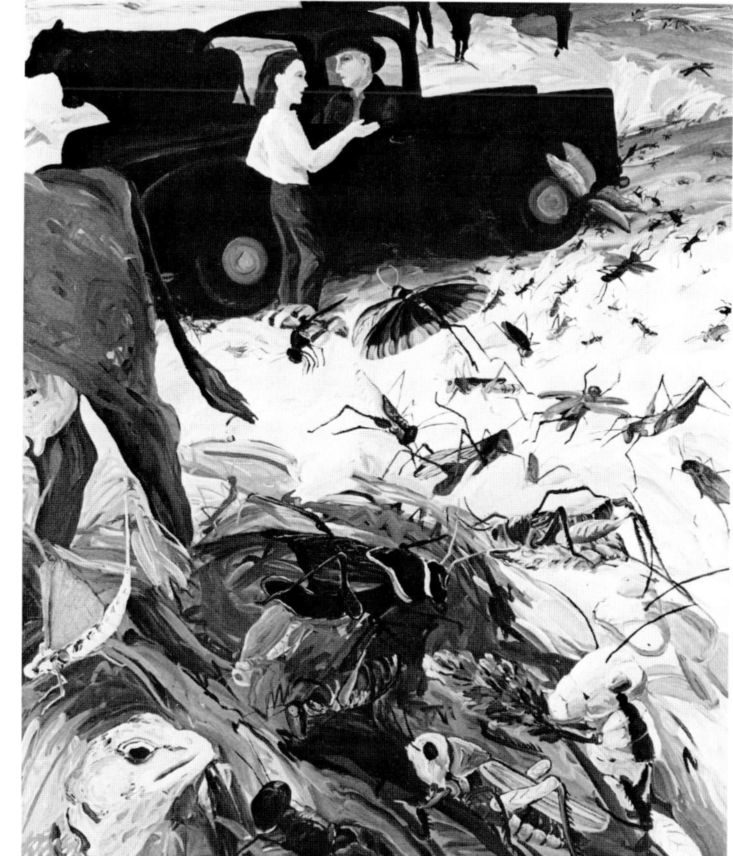

Talking to Eddie, 1979
oil on canvas
48 x 40″
Collection Basil N. Scaljon and
F. Lynne Wilkerson, San Antonio

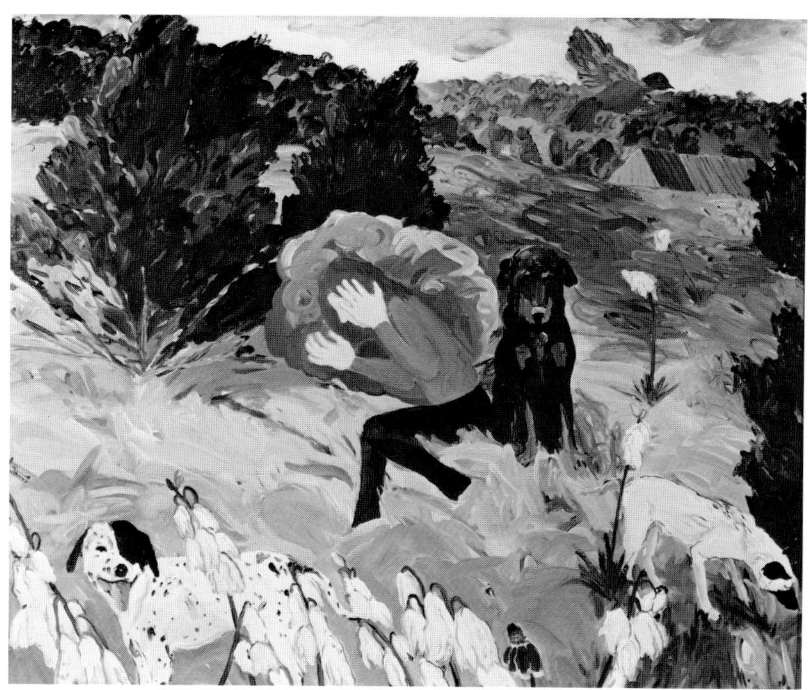

The Black Cloud, 1979
oil on canvas
30 x 36″
Collection the artist

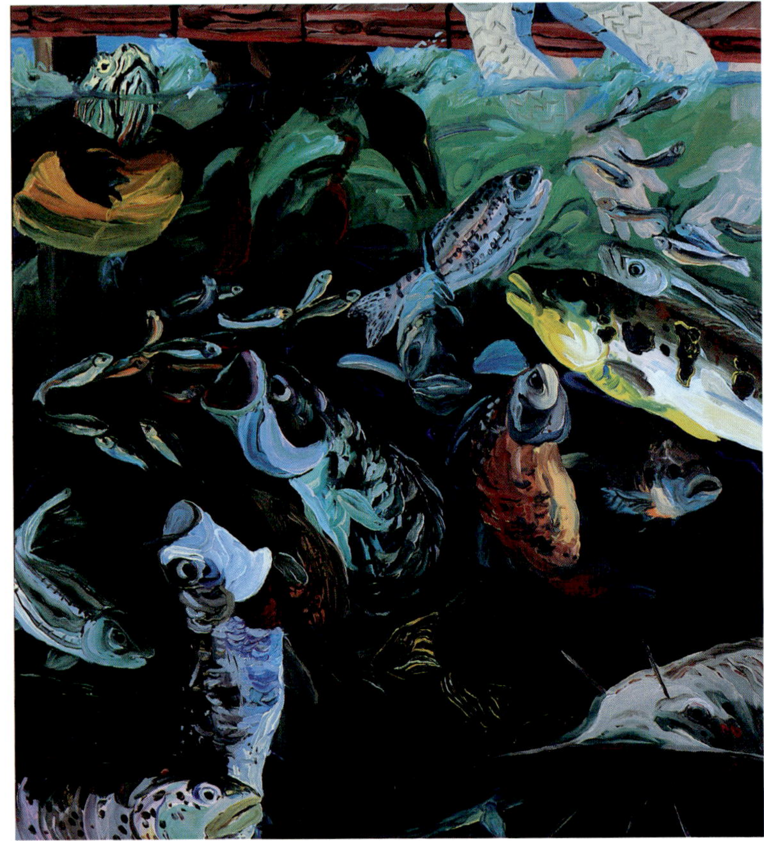

Crowded Lake, 1979
oil on canvas
50 x 44"
Collection Mrs. Vernon L. Miller

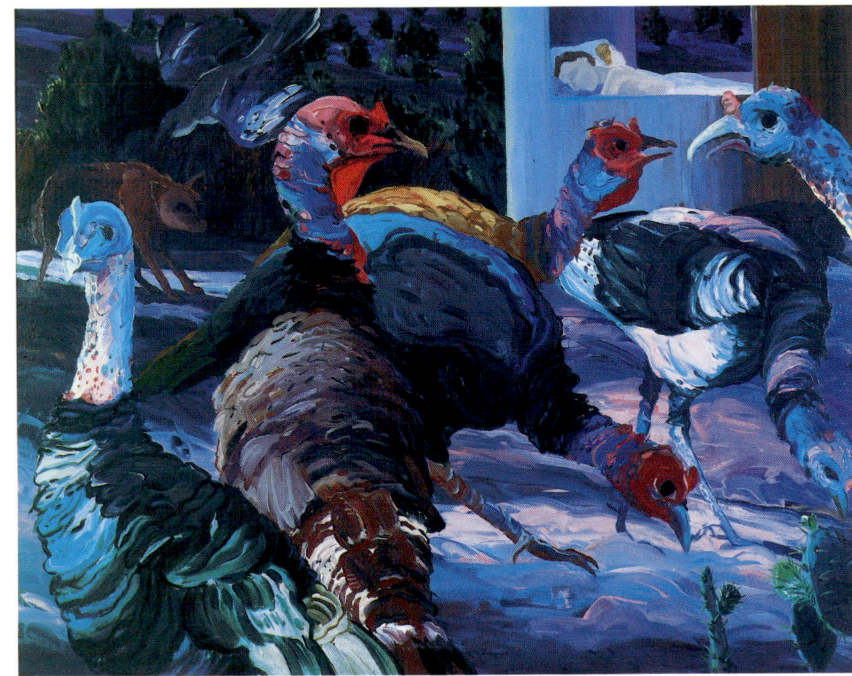

Meeting at Dawn, 1979
oil on canvas
40 x 50"
Collection Dr. M. Marjorie Menefee

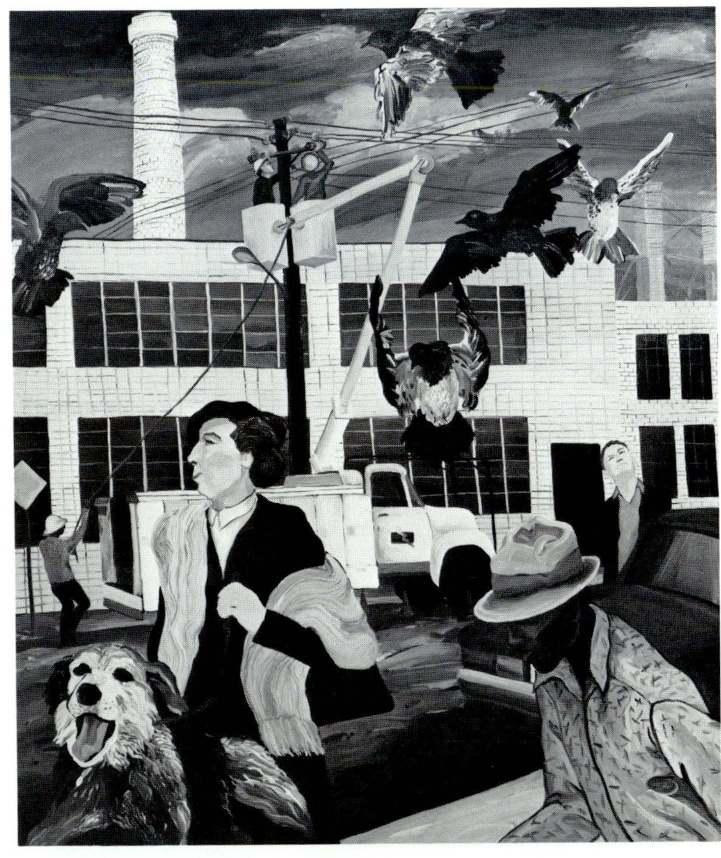

Studio Building, 1980
oil on canvas
52 x 44"
Collection Mr. and Mrs. William H.H. Rees

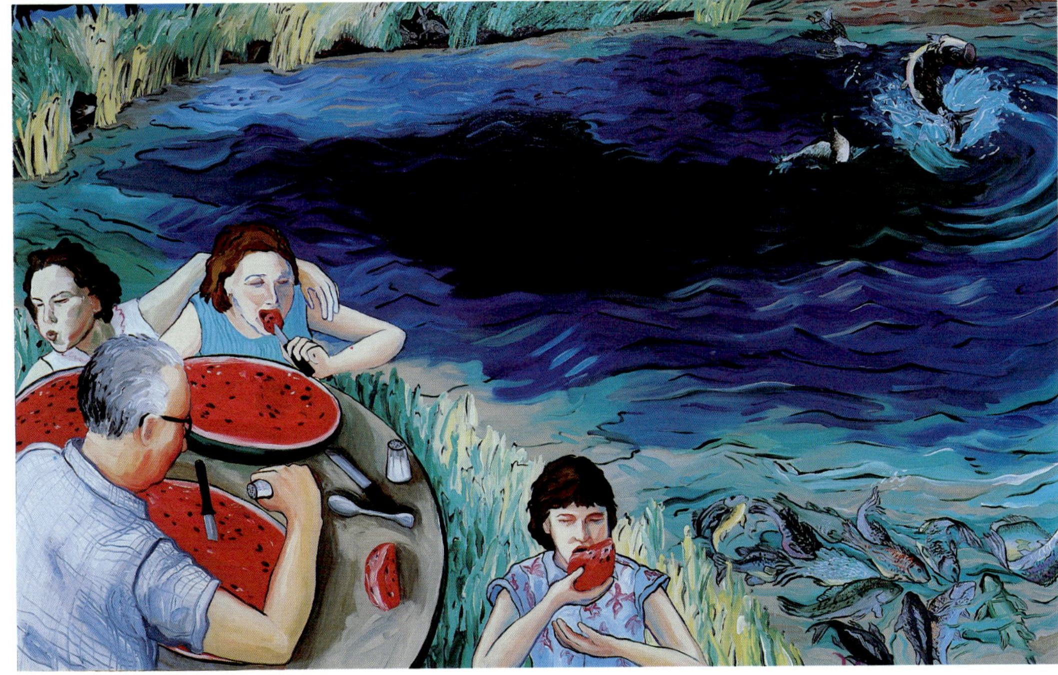

The Splash, 1980
oil on canvas
40 x 60"
Collection Wayland and Ruth Brill

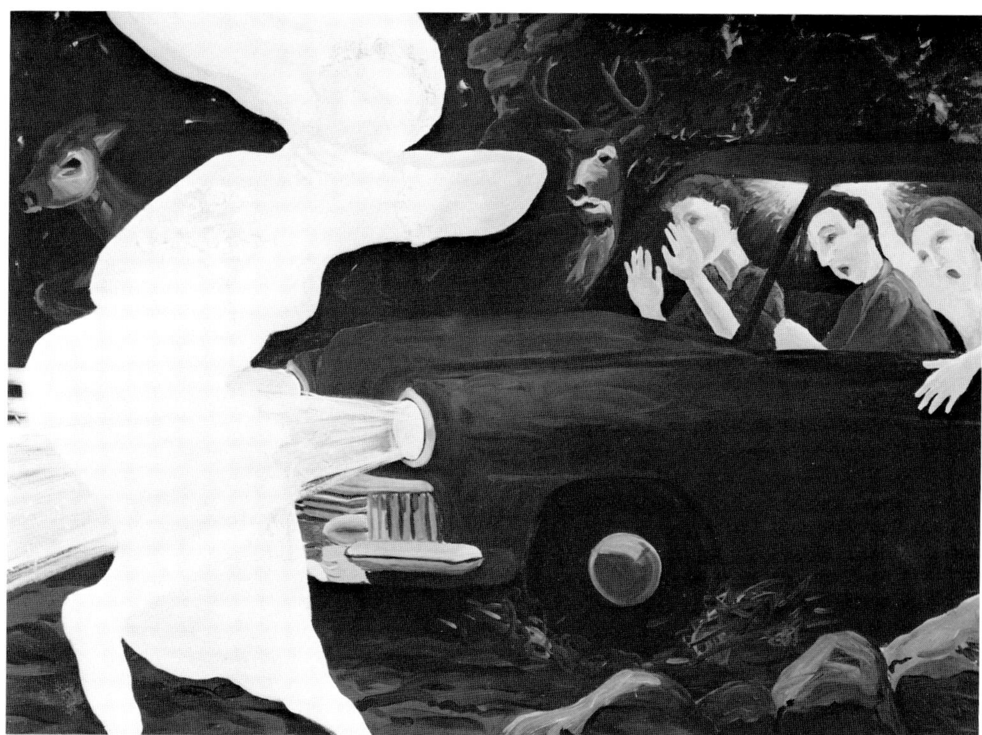

The Ghost of Bride's Camp, 1979
oil on canvas
28 x 38″
Collection the artist

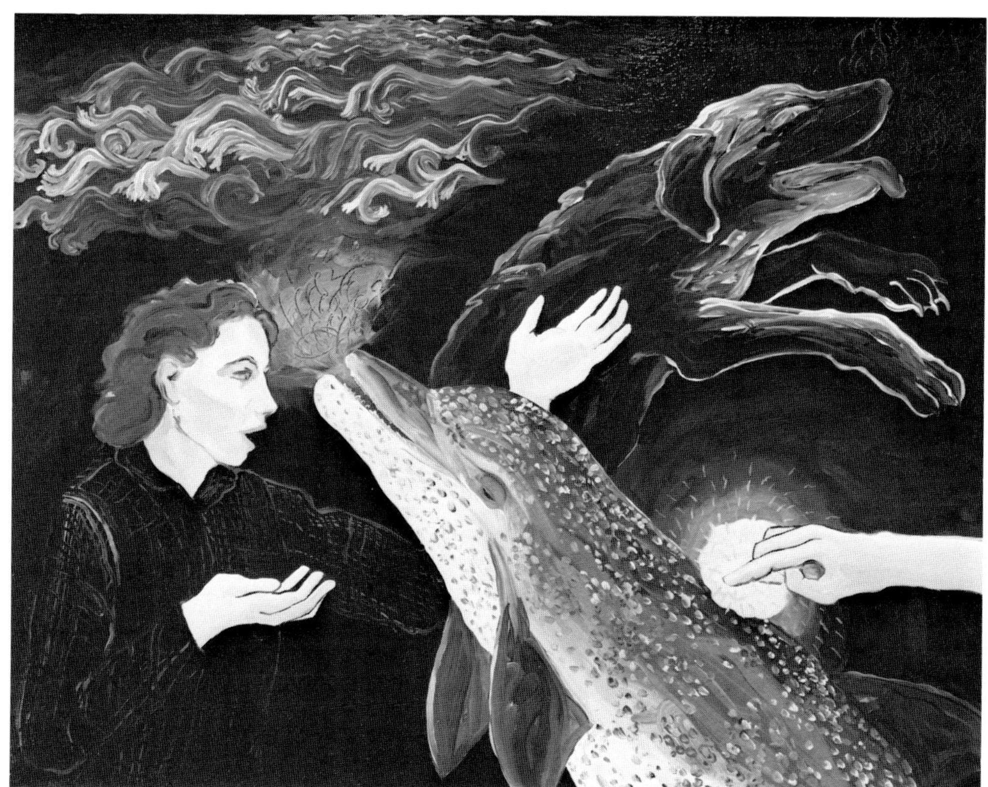

Dream of a Dolphin Who Was Really My Dog, 1980
oil on canvas
30 x 38″
Collection the artist

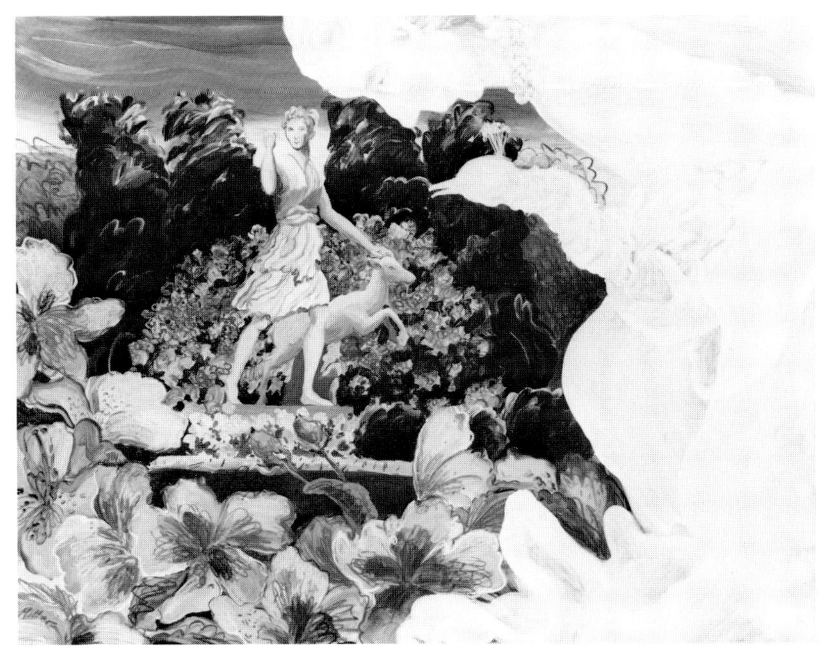

Miss Ima Visits Diana, 1981
acrylic on paper
22 x 29″
Collection AMOCO Production Company

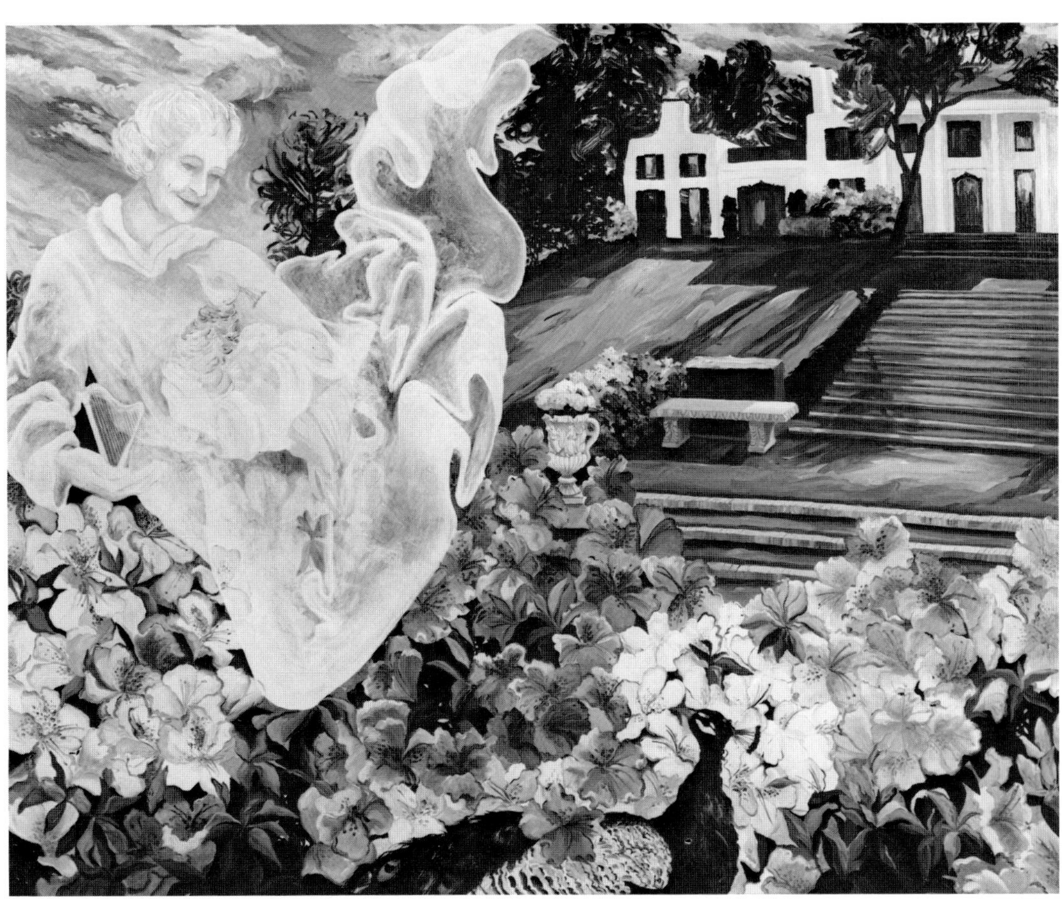

The Generous Spirit of Miss Ima, 1981
oil on canvas
50 x 60″
Collection the artist

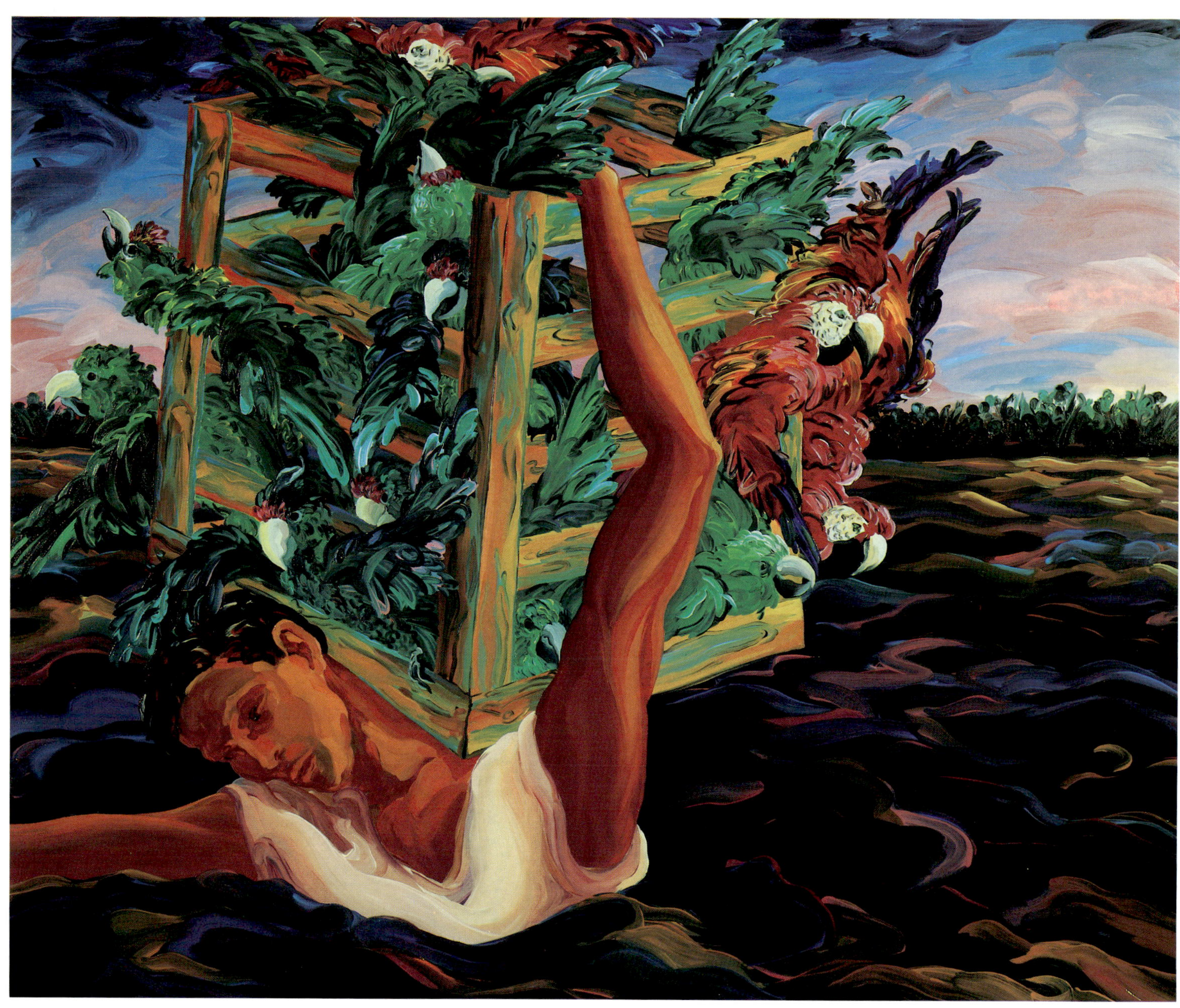

Smuggling Parrots Across the Border, 1981
oil on canvas
42×50″
Collection Malou Flato and John Taliaferro

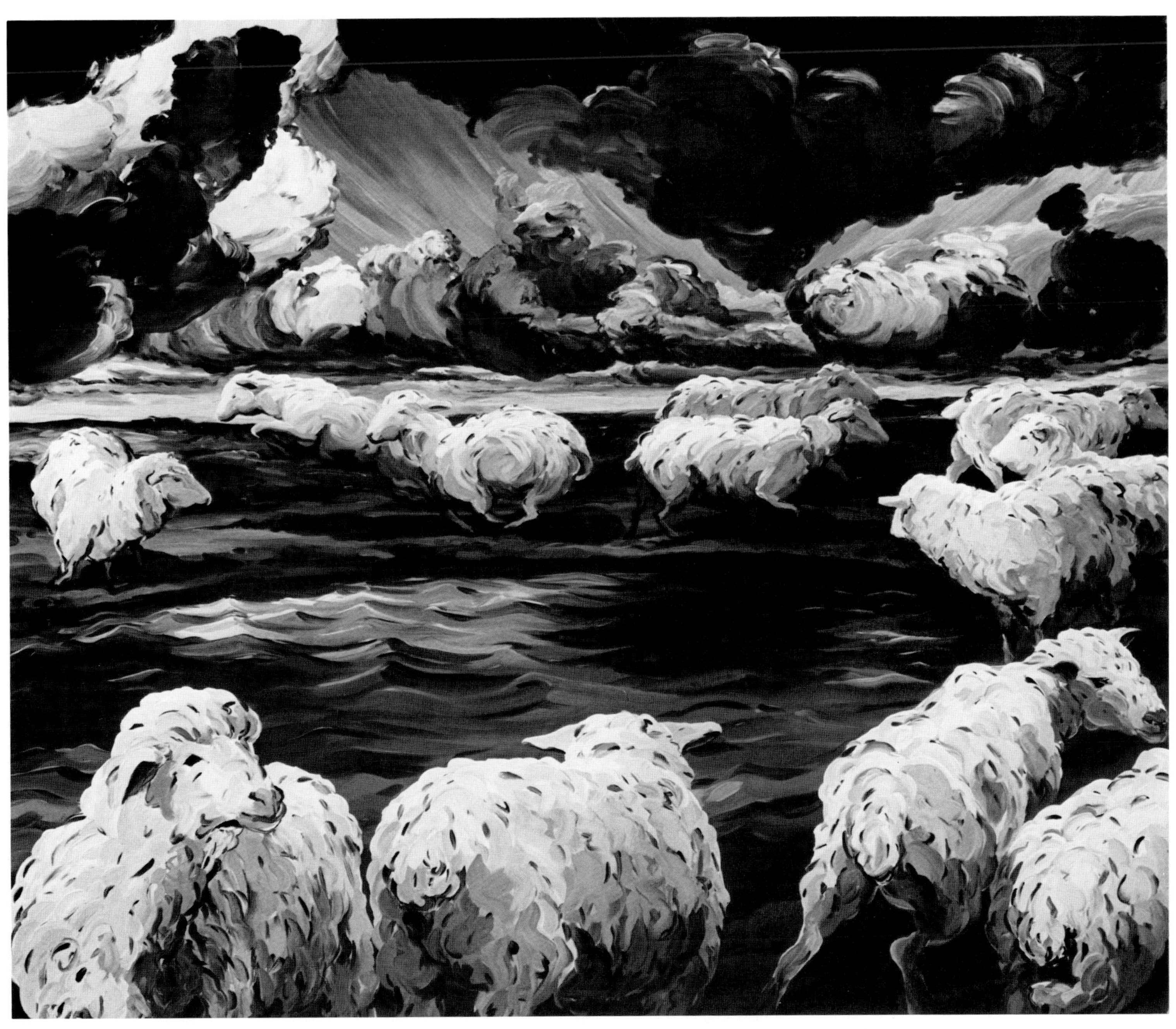

Tempesta, 1981
oil on canvas
54 x 62″
Collection Mr. and Mrs. Oliver R. Mattingly

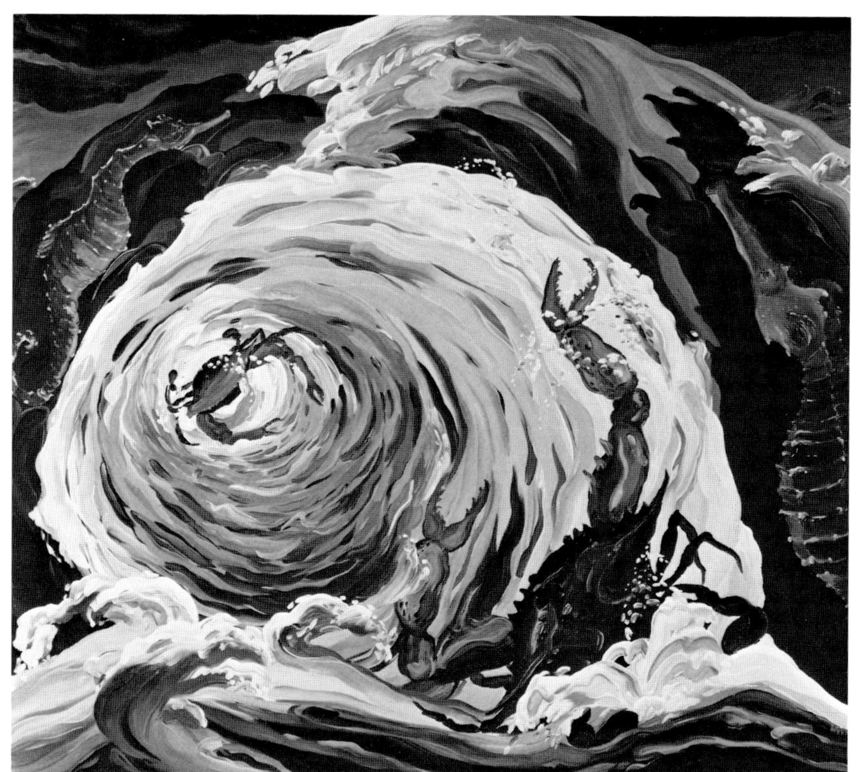

Undertow, 1981
oil on linen
38 x 42½″
Collection Dr. and Mrs. Earl Koile

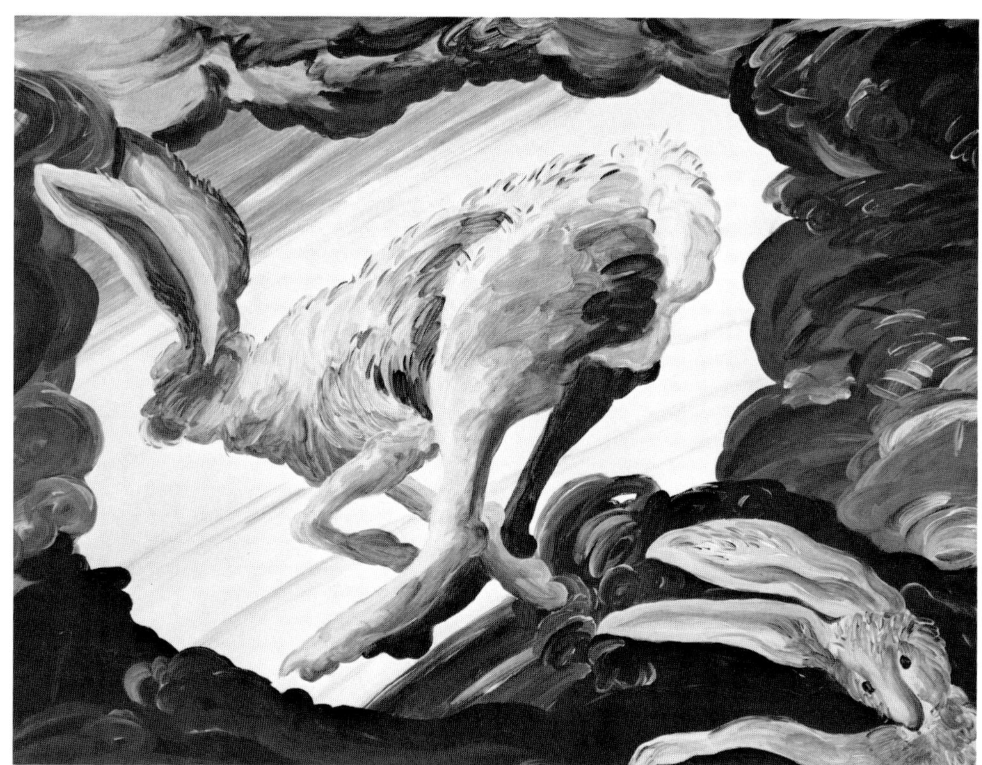

Studies for the Ark: Eye of the Storm, 1981
acrylic on paper
24 x 30″
Collection Sherry L. Bryan

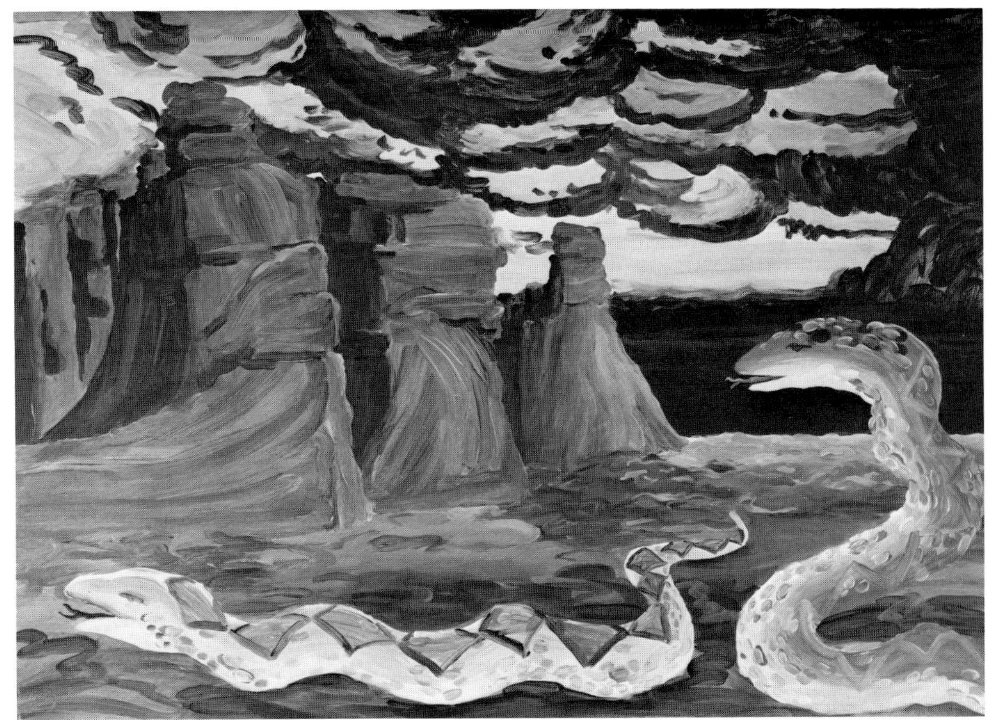

Studies for the Ark: Snakes, 1981
acrylic on paper
23 x 29″
Collection Atlantic Richfield Company,
Corporate Art Collection

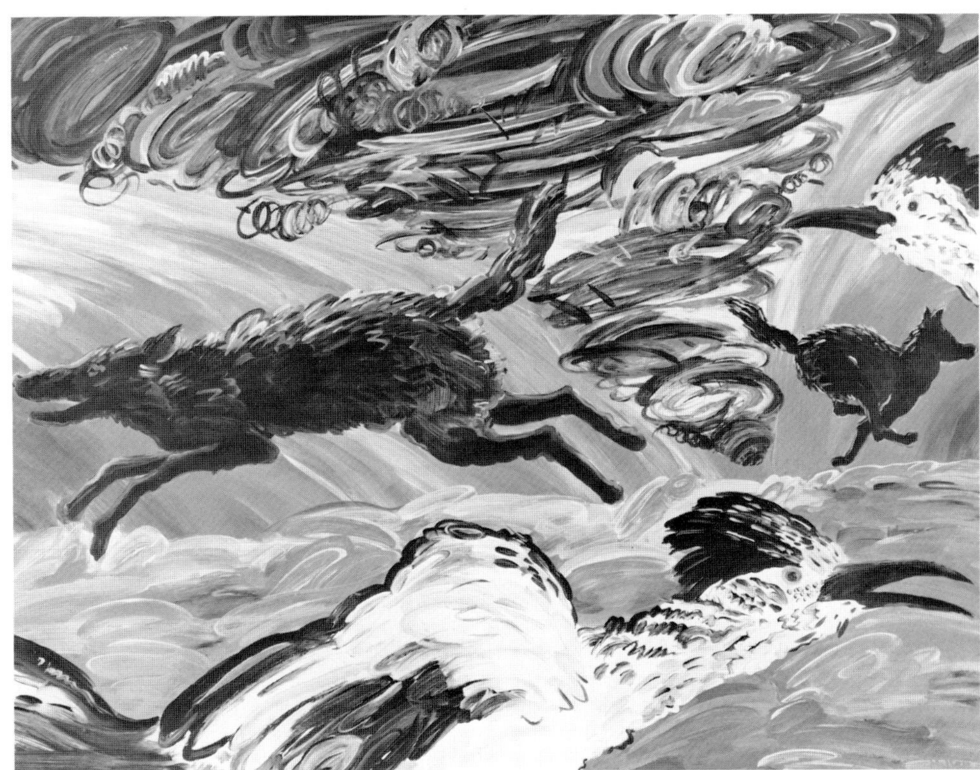

**Studies for the Ark:
Coyotes and Roadrunners,** 1981
acrylic on paper
23 x 29″
Private Collection, Dallas

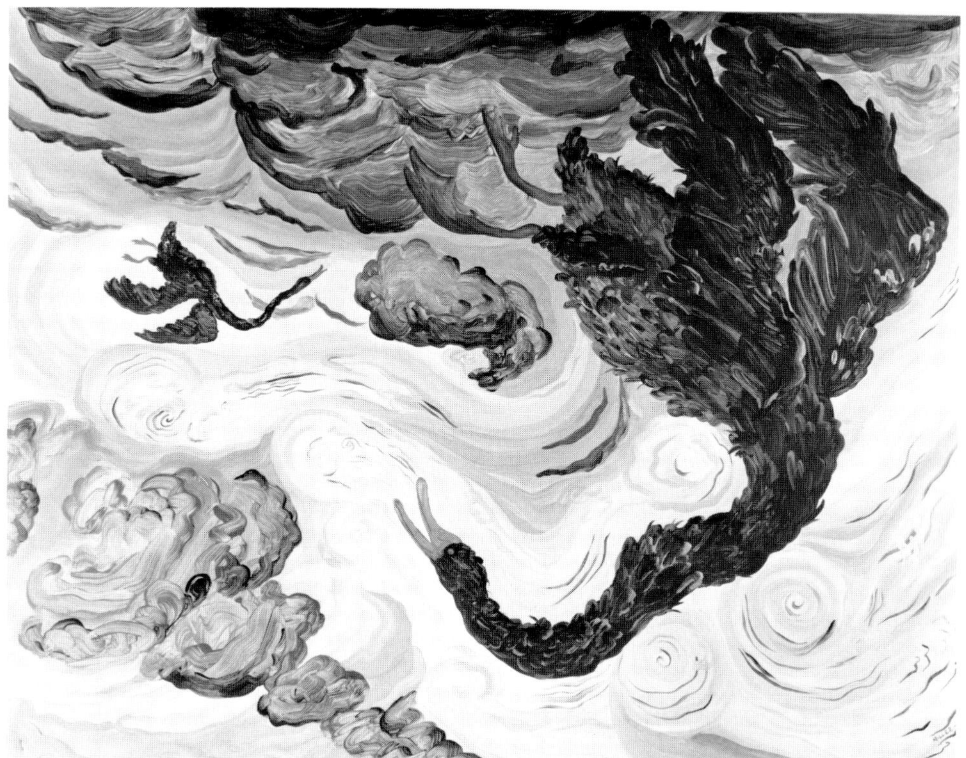

Studies for the Ark: Black Swans, 1981
acrylic on paper
23 x 29″
Collection Mr. and Mrs. Edward Spevack,
Huntington, New York

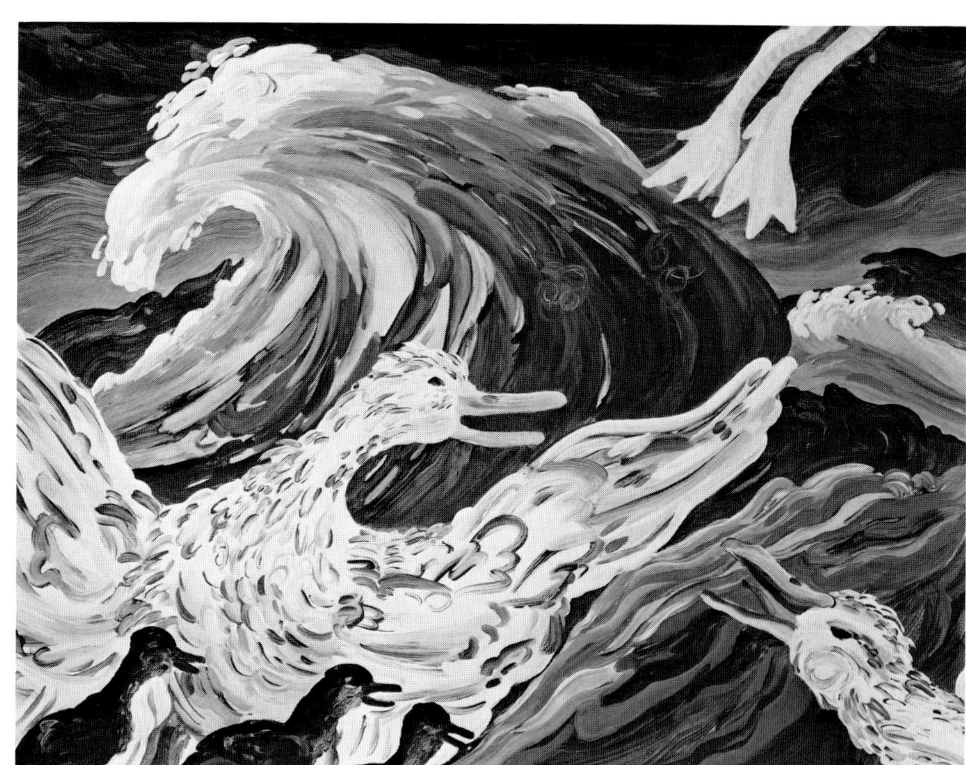

Studies for the Ark: Ducks, 1981
acrylic on paper
23 x 29″
Collection Dr. M. Marjorie Menefee

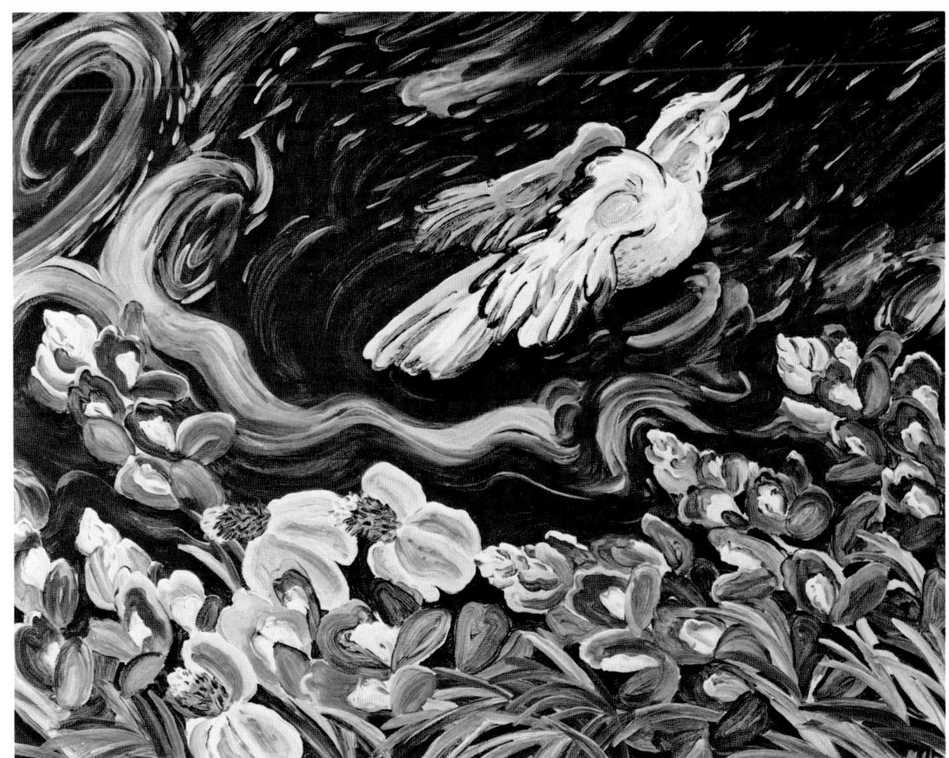

Studies for the Ark: Bird Against the Wind, 1981
acrylic on paper
23 x 29"
Collection Bill and Janet Kennedy, Austin

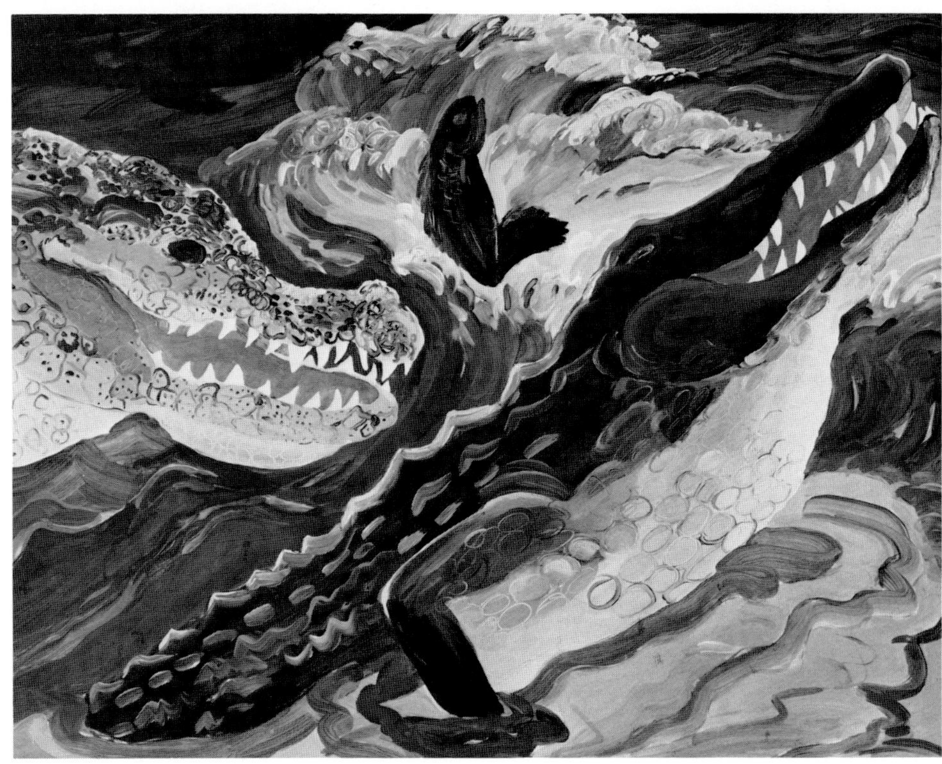

Studies for the Ark: Alligators, 1981
acrylic on paper
23 x 29"
Collection Polly Little and Mark Lavatelli

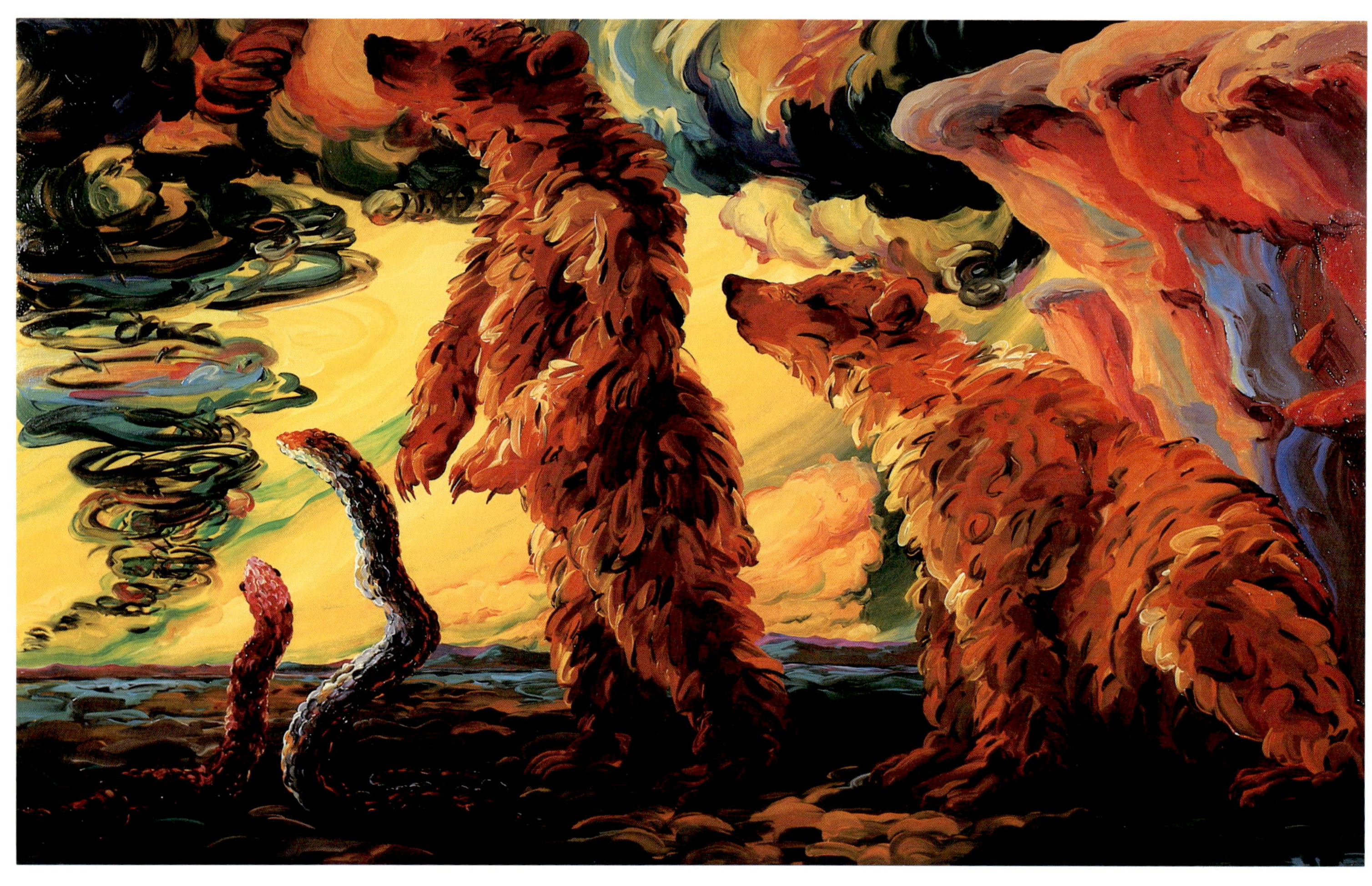

Anticipation, 1981
oil on canvas
50 x 80"
Collection Mrs. Vernon L. Miller

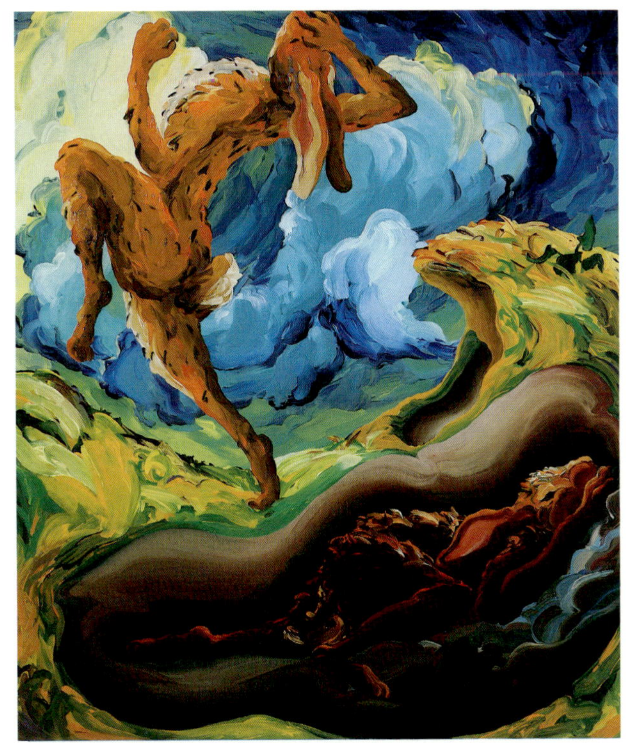

One Rabbit Feeling the Pain of Another, 1982
oil on linen
50 x 42"
Collection Betty Moody and Bill Steffy

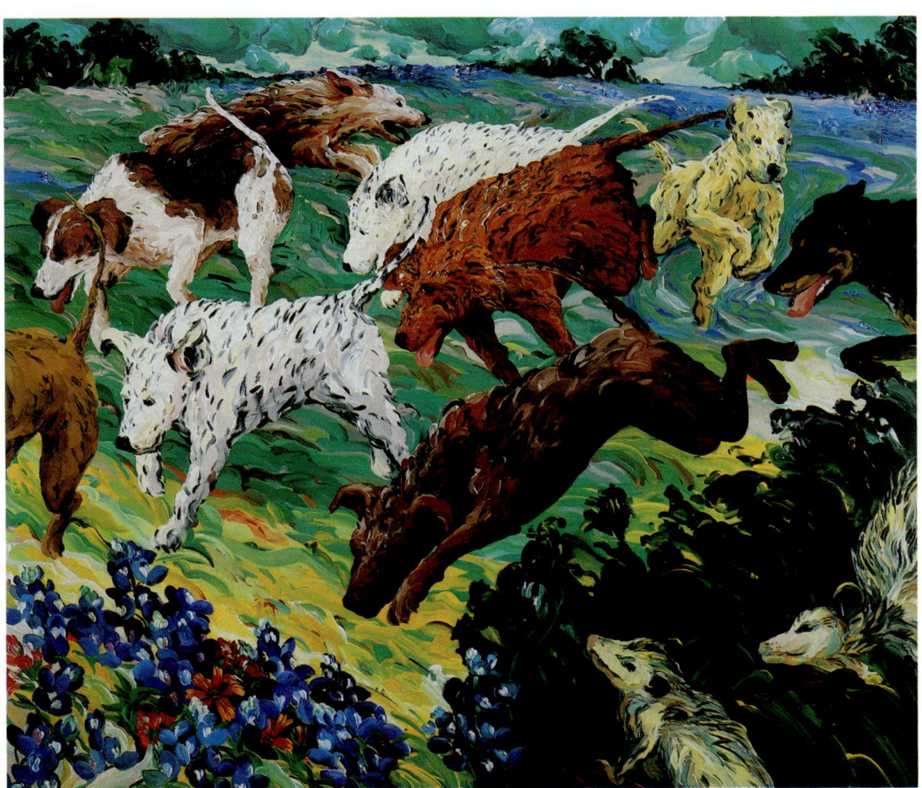

Pack and Possums, 1982
oil on canvas
54 x 64"
Collection Mr. and Mrs. Roy S. O'Connor, Houston

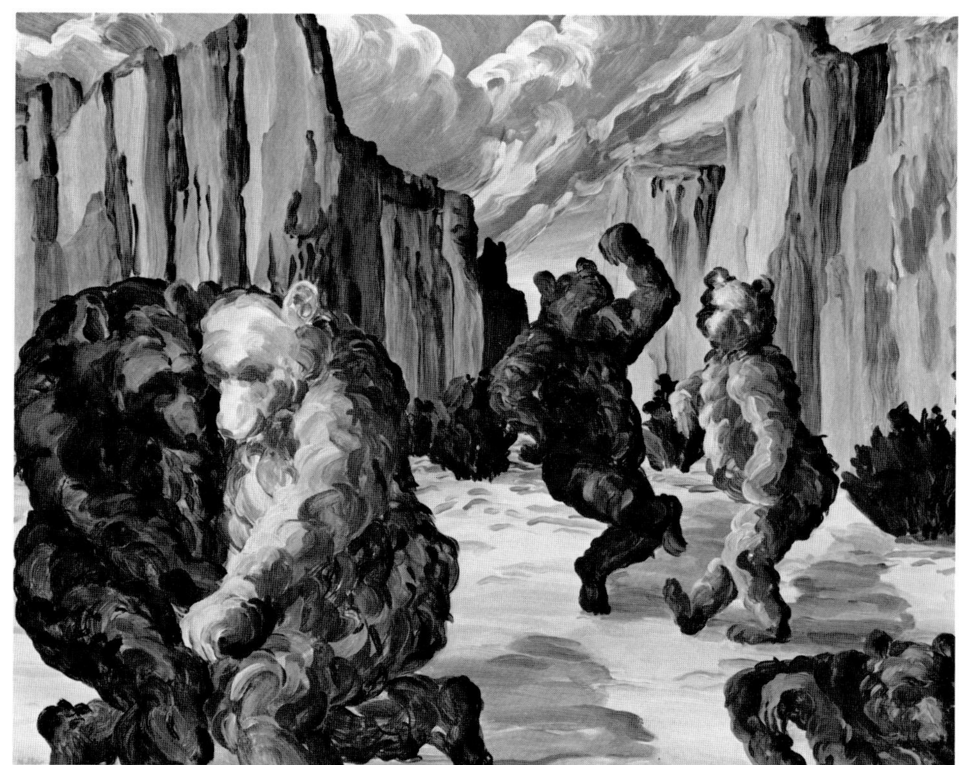

Bear Dance in Canyon, 1982
acrylic on paper
23 x 29″
Collection Dr. and Mrs. Stephen A. Szygenda

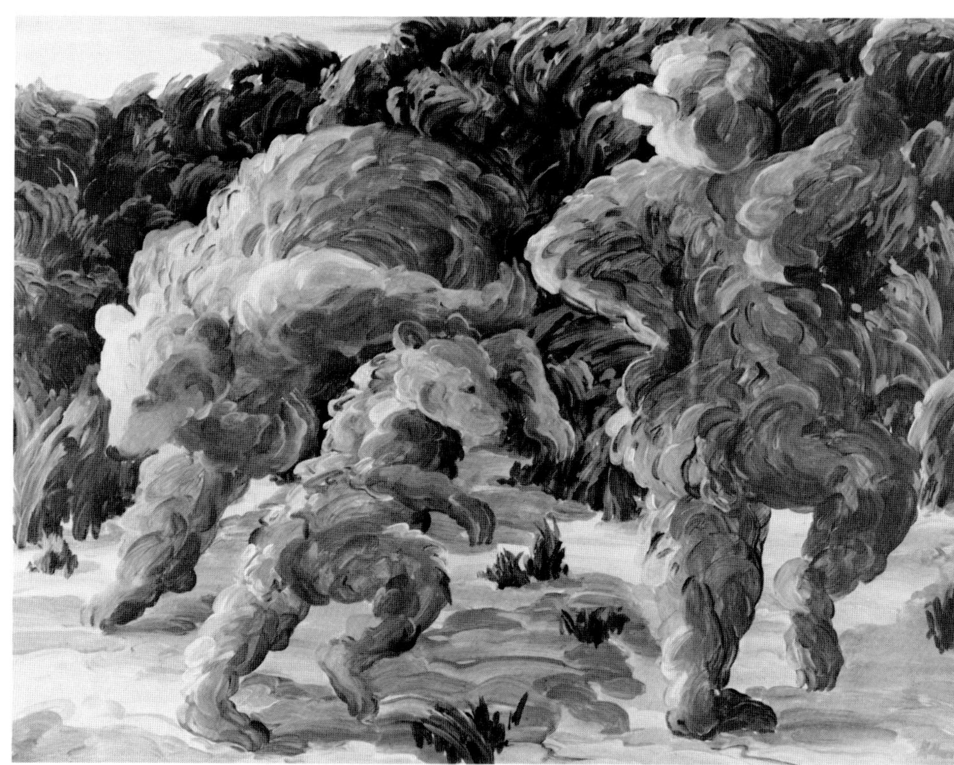

Bear Dance in Clearing, 1982
acrylic on paper
22 x 28″
Collection Atlantic Richfield Company,
Corporate Art Collection

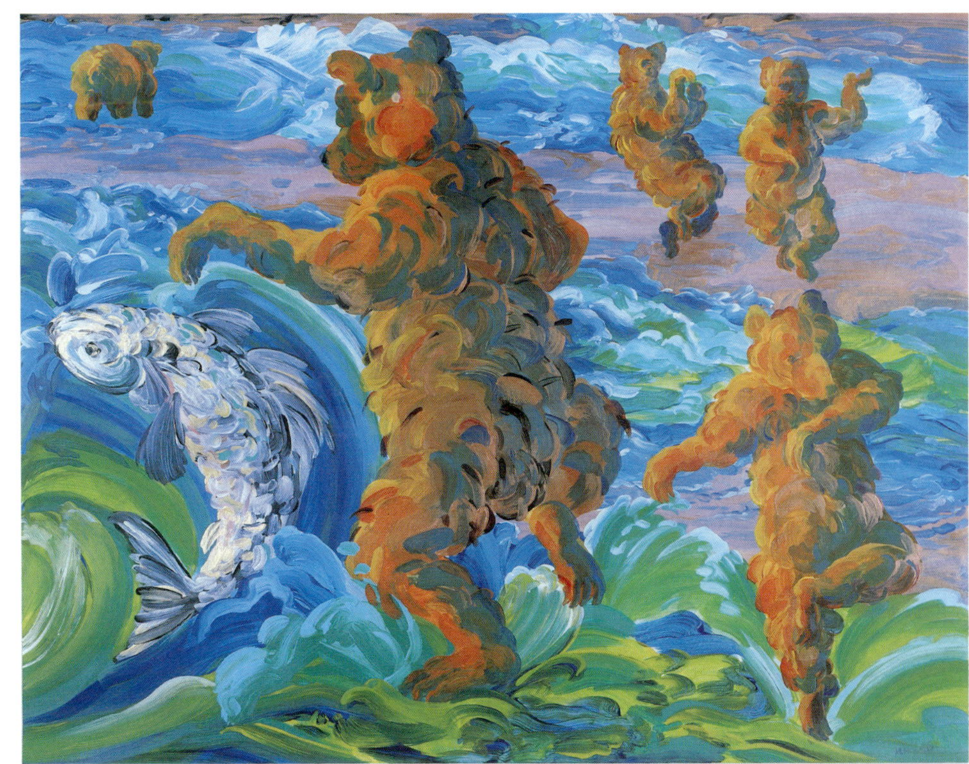

Bear Dance in River, 1982
acrylic on paper
23 x 29″
Private Collection, Houston

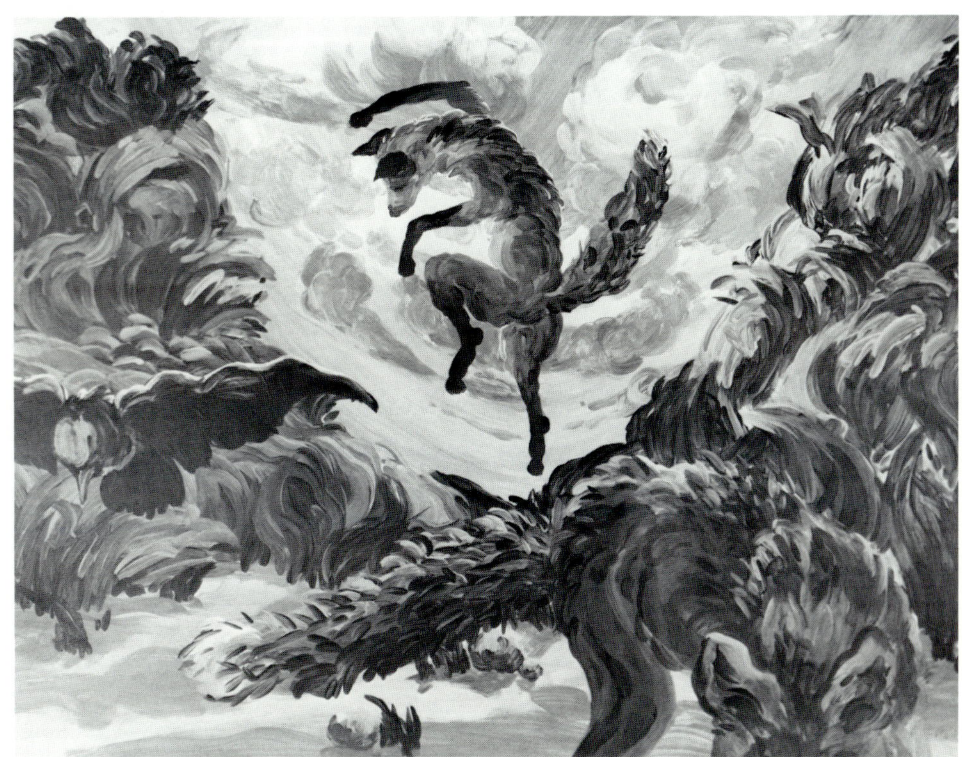

Fox Dance at Dusk, 1982
acrylic on paper
23 x 29″
Bob Butler and Sonny Burt, Dallas

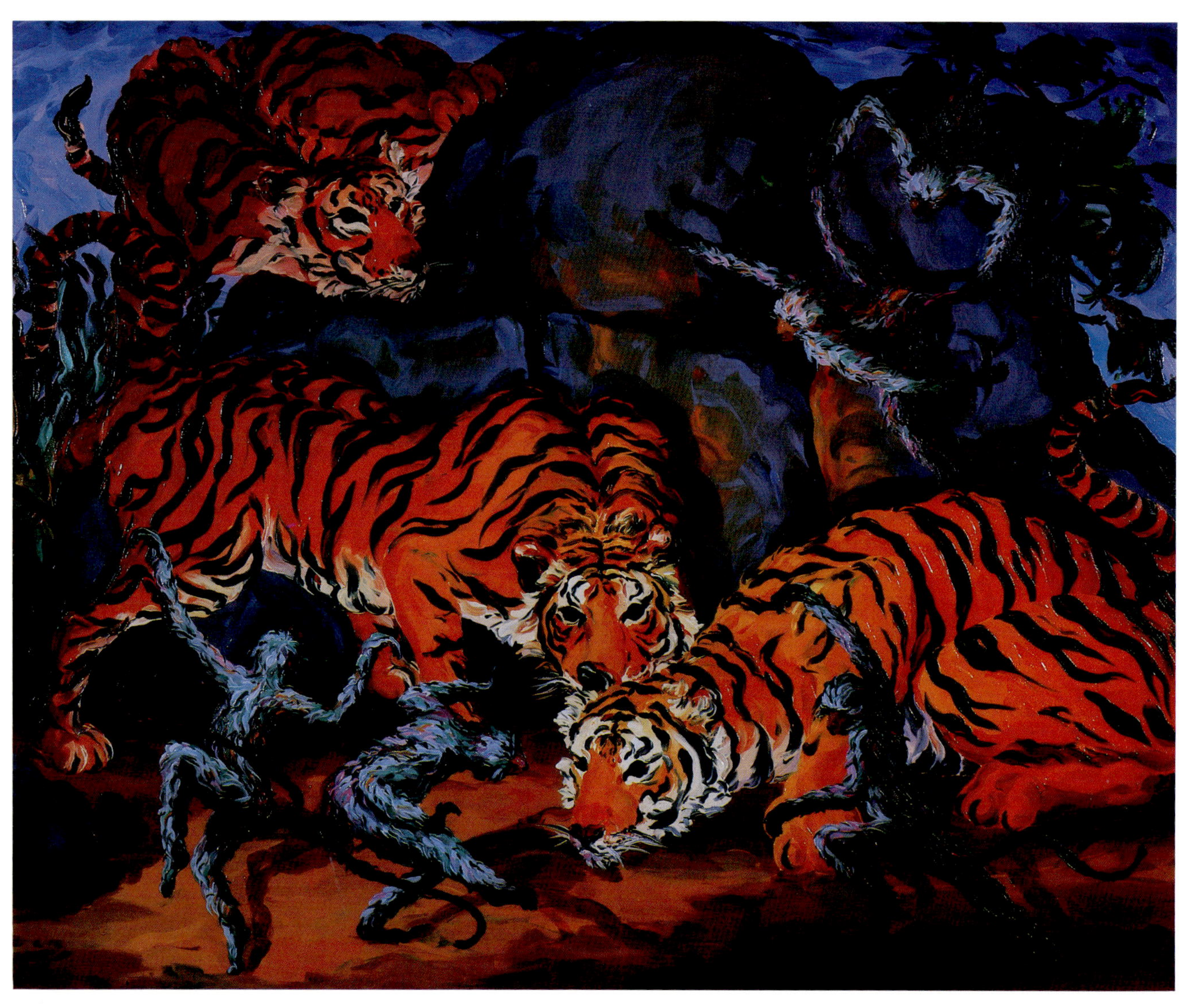

Untitled (Tigers), 1982
oil on canvas
58 x 70"
Collection Bob Wilson

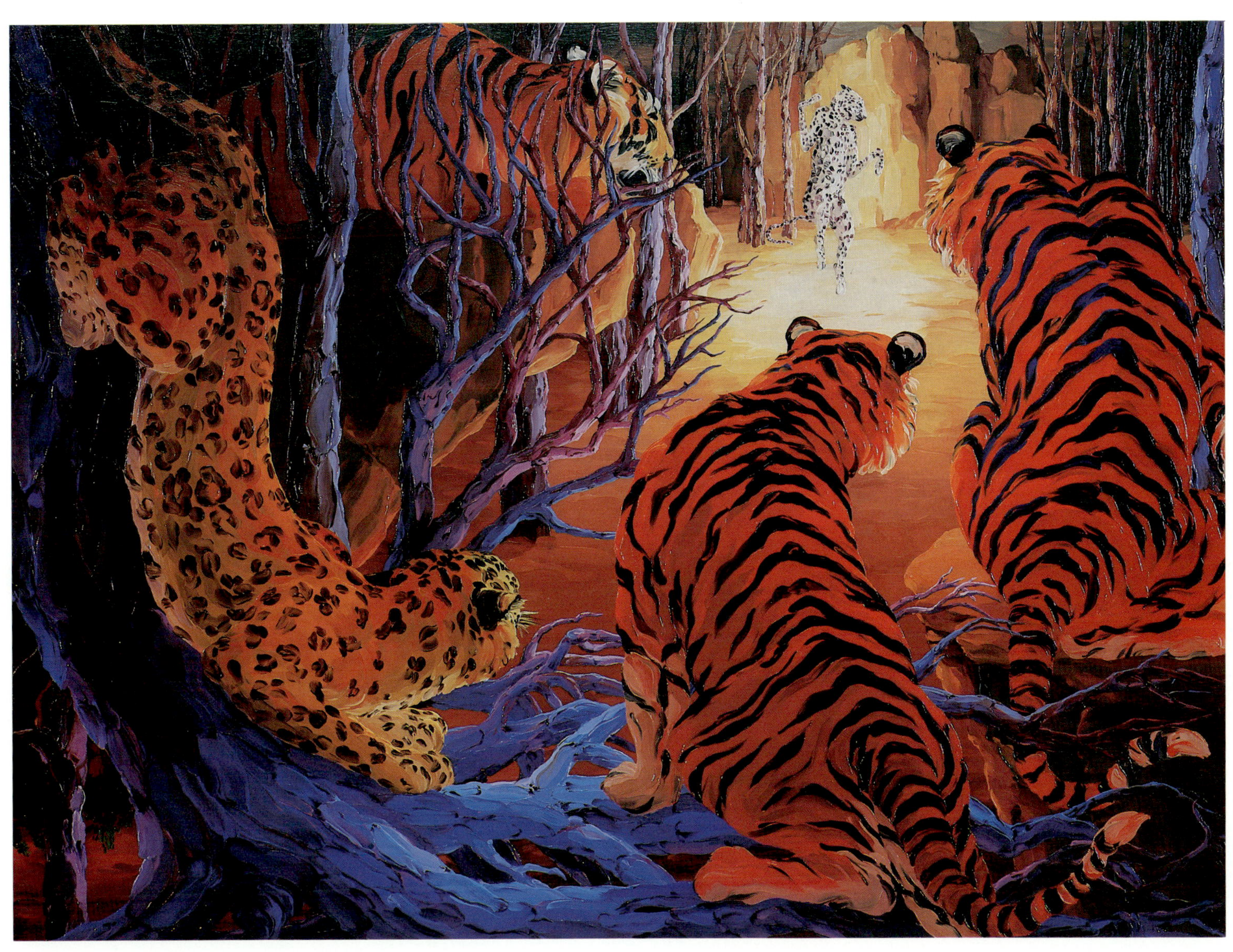

Leopard Dance, 1983
oil on linen
60 x 80"
Private Collection, Houston

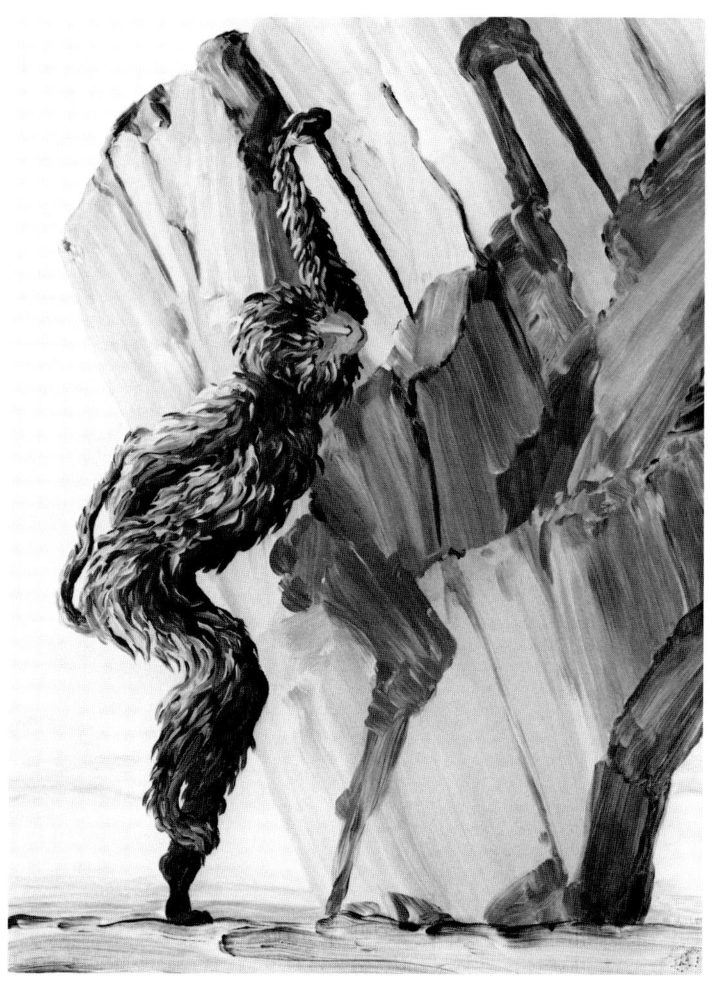

Stork Shadow, 1983
acrylic on paper
30 x 22″
Collection Mr. and Mrs. A.L. Ballard

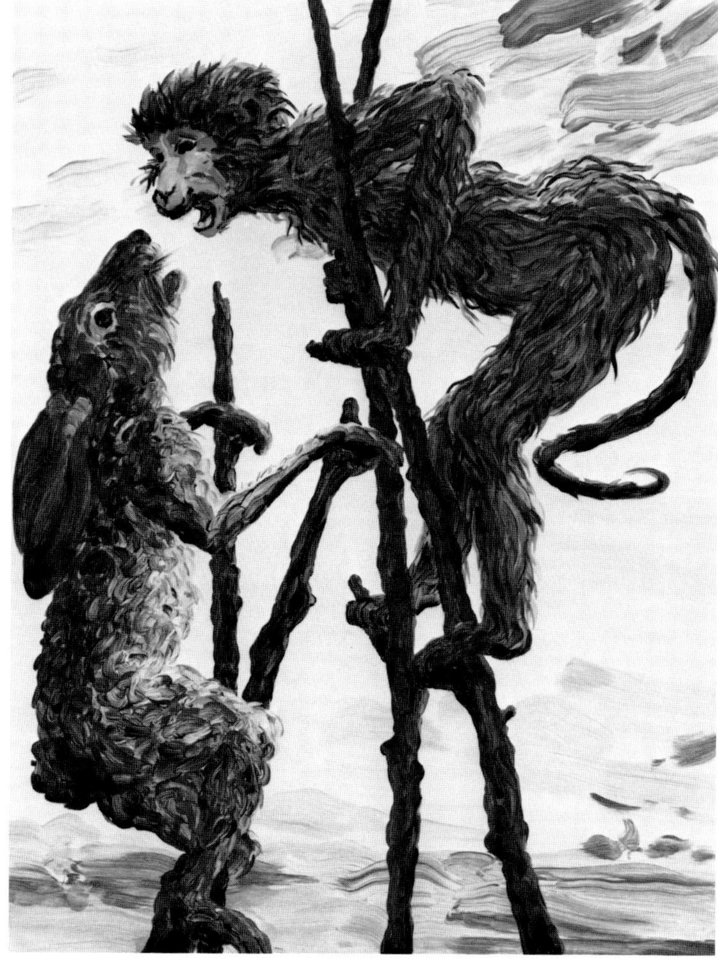

Conversation on Stilts, 1983
acrylic on paper
30 x 22″
Collection The First National Bank of Chicago

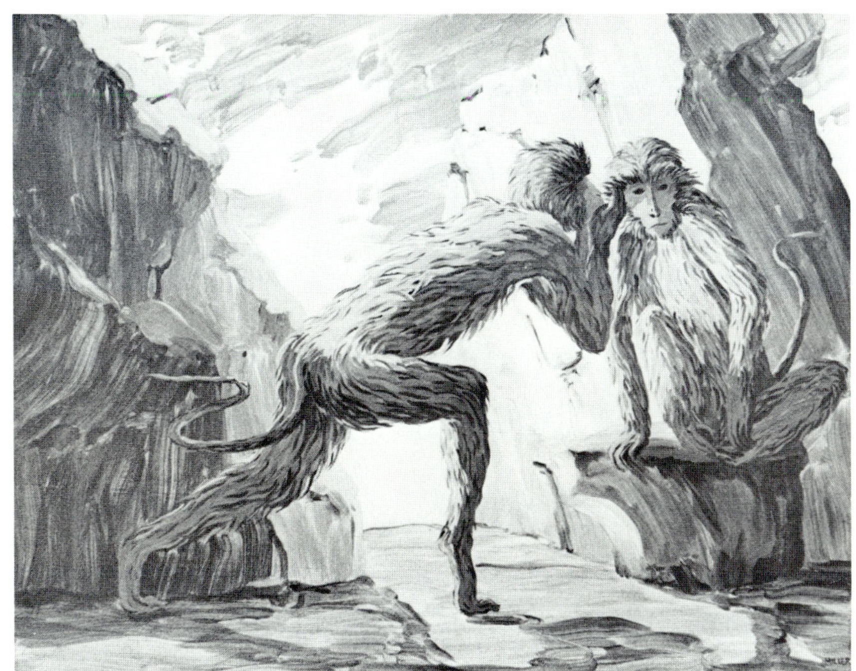

Secret, 1984
acrylic on paper
22 x 30″
Collection Don Blaustein

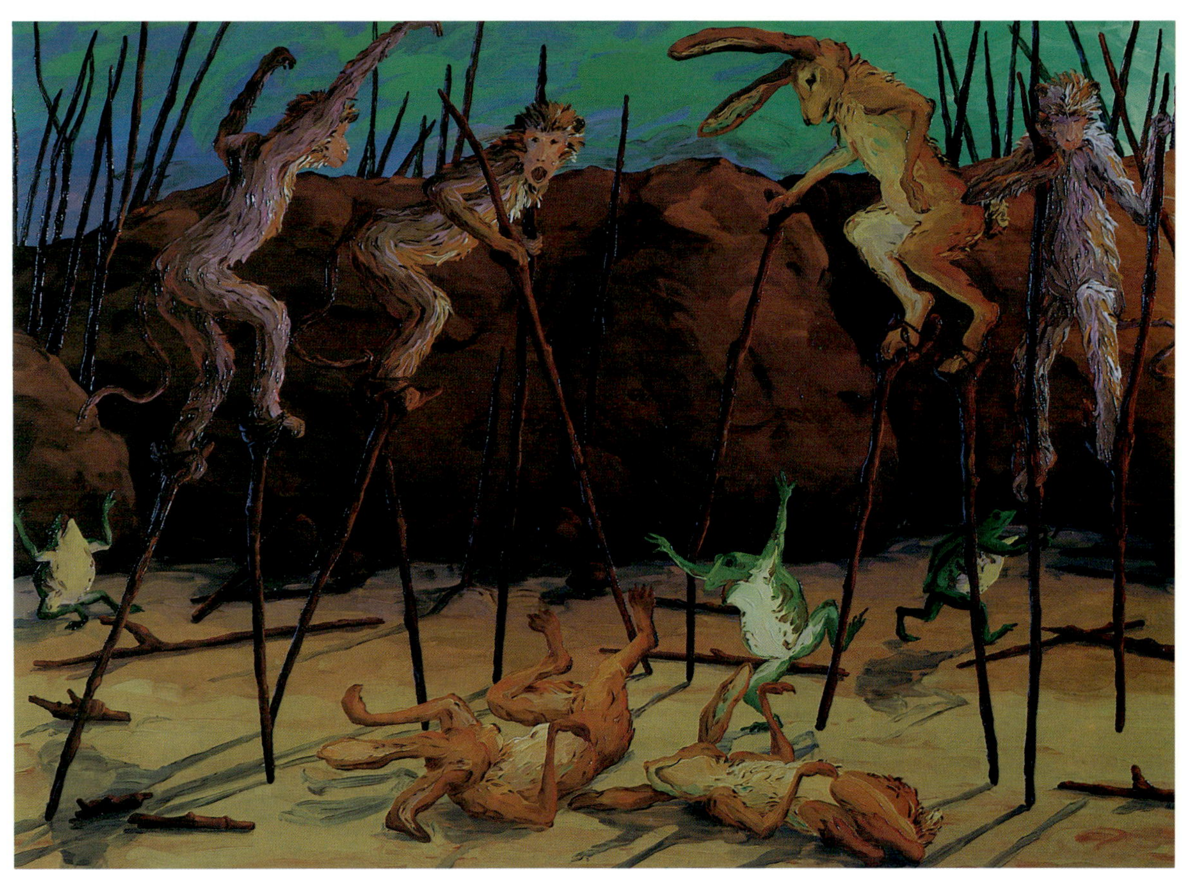

Clowns, 1983
oil on linen
56 x 76″
Collection Mr. and Mrs. I.H. Kempner III

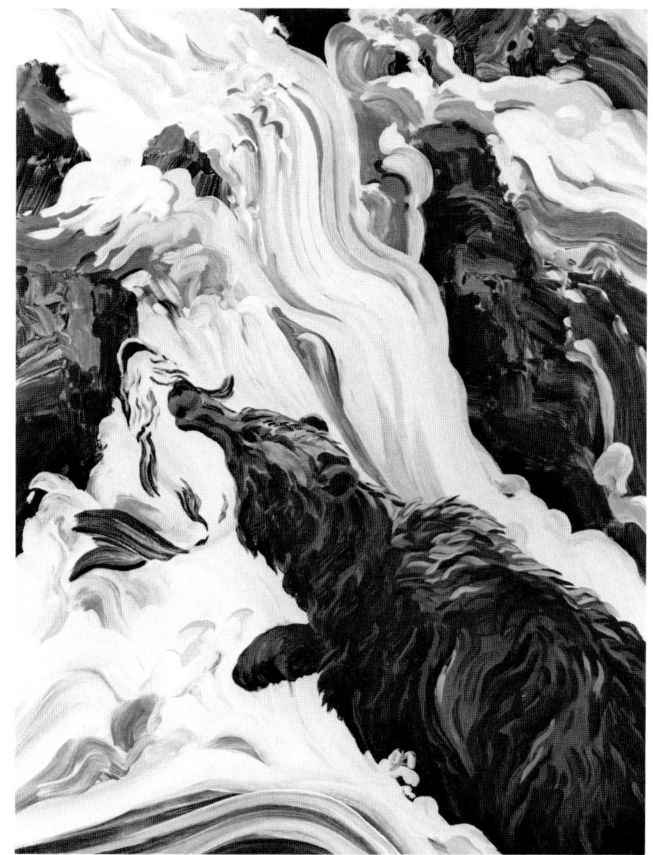

Orange Bear, 1983
acrylic on paper
30 x 22″
Collection Ms. Kenny Griffith Baldwin, Houston, Texas

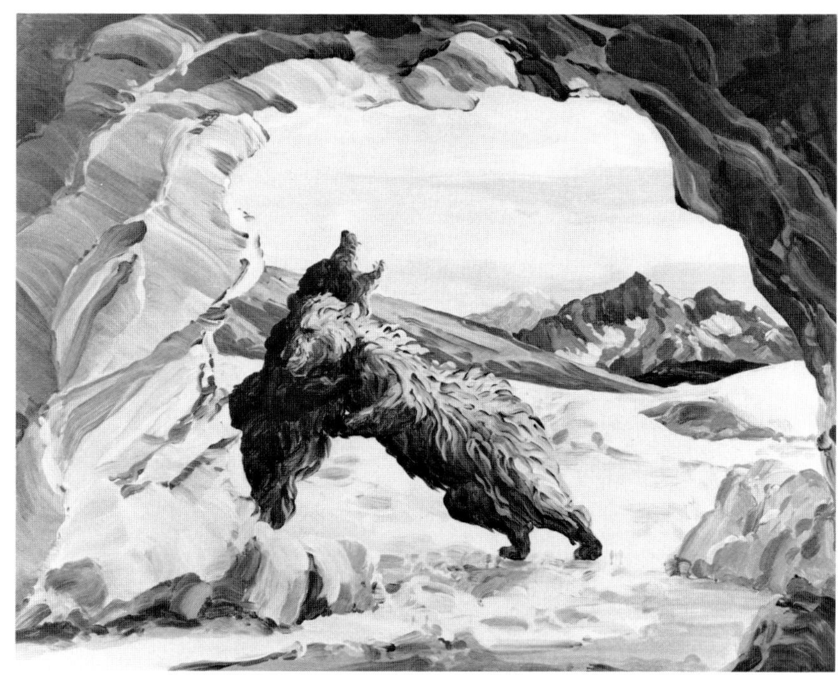

Ice Cave, 1983
acrylic on paper
23 x 29″
Collection Anne S. Dayton

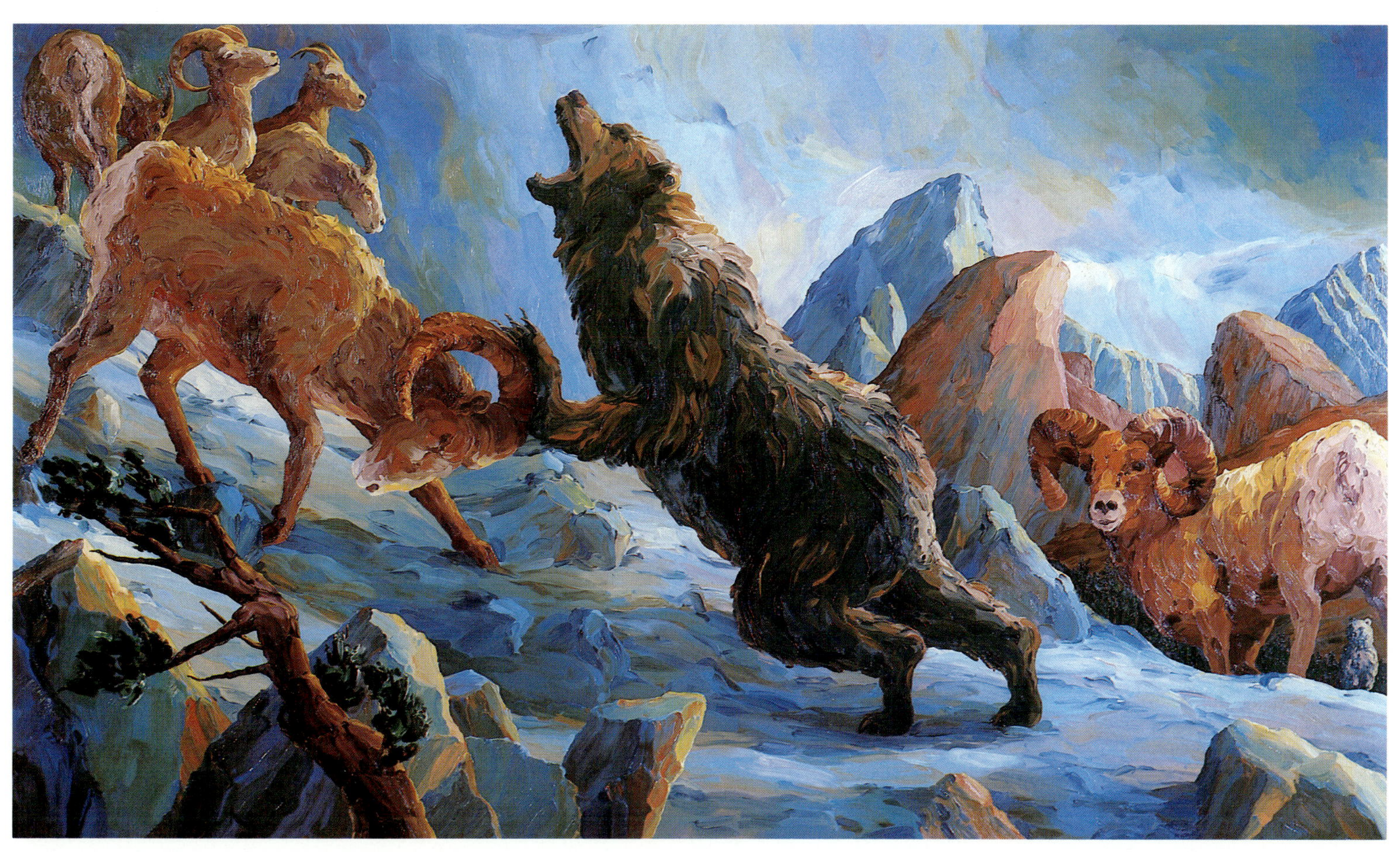

Territory, 1983
oil on linen
69 x 116″
Collection PaineWebber Group Inc.

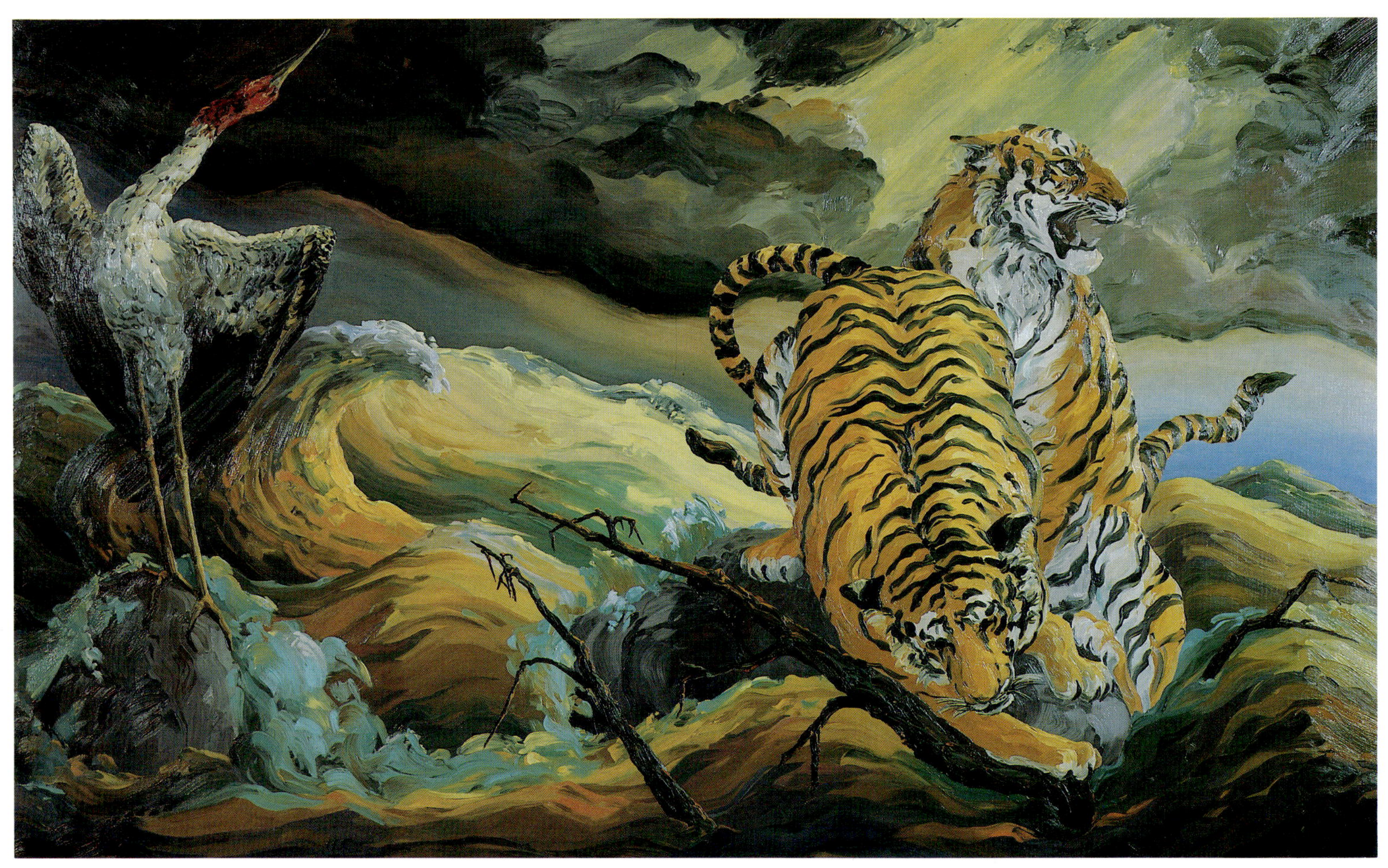

Flood, 1983
oil on linen
59 x 95″
Collection The Museum of Fine Arts, Houston.
Museum purchase with funds from
Texas Eastern Corporation

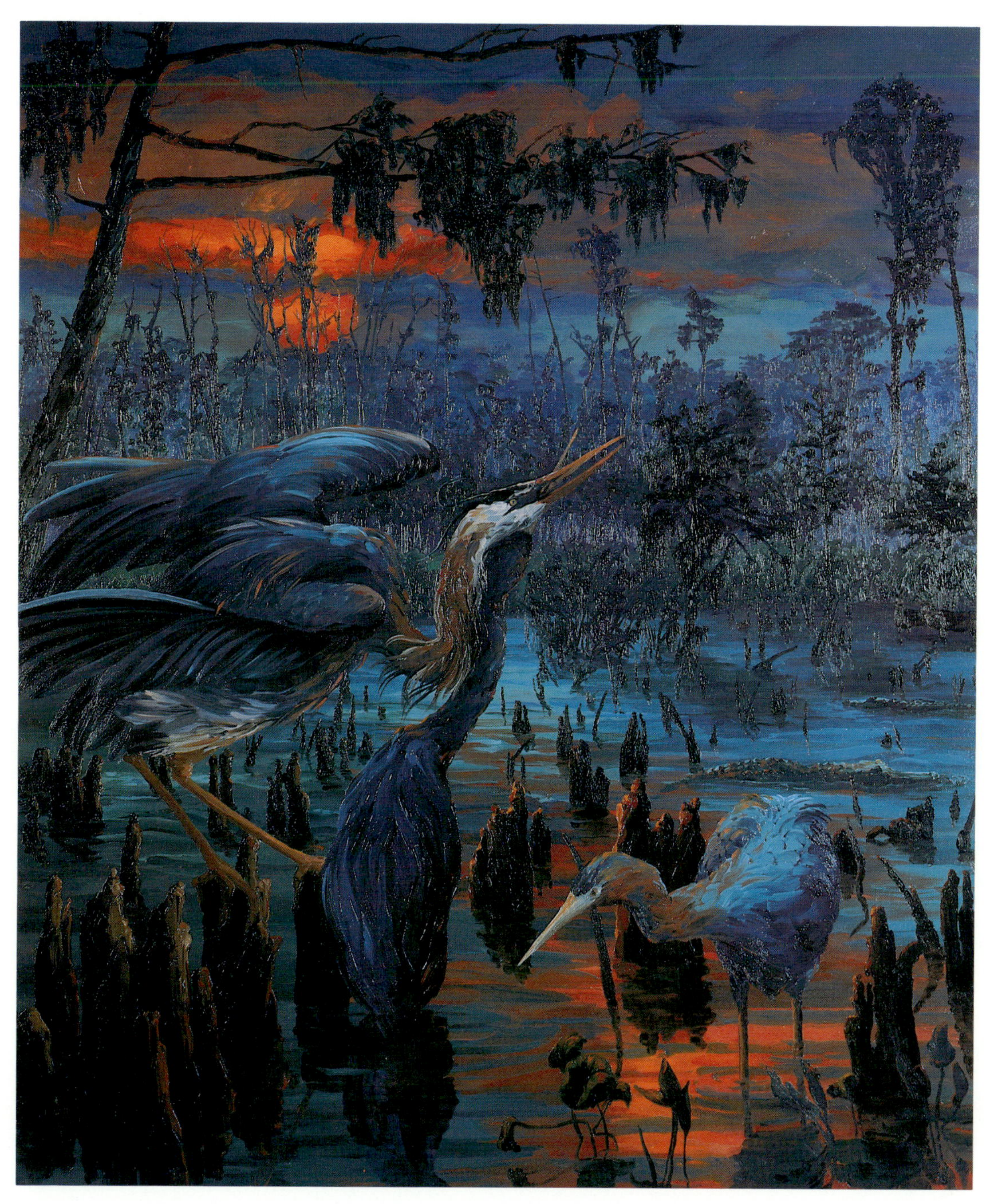

Swamp, 1983
oil on linen
72 x 59″
Collection Holly Solomon, New York

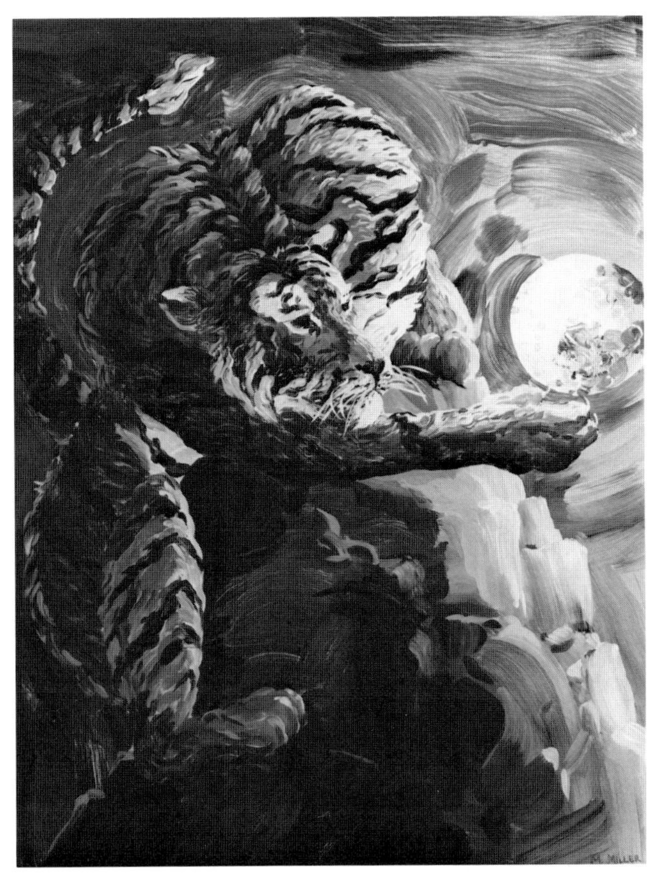

Swatting the Moon, 1983
acrylic on paper
29 x 22″
Collection Mr. and Mrs. Roy S. O'Connor, Houston

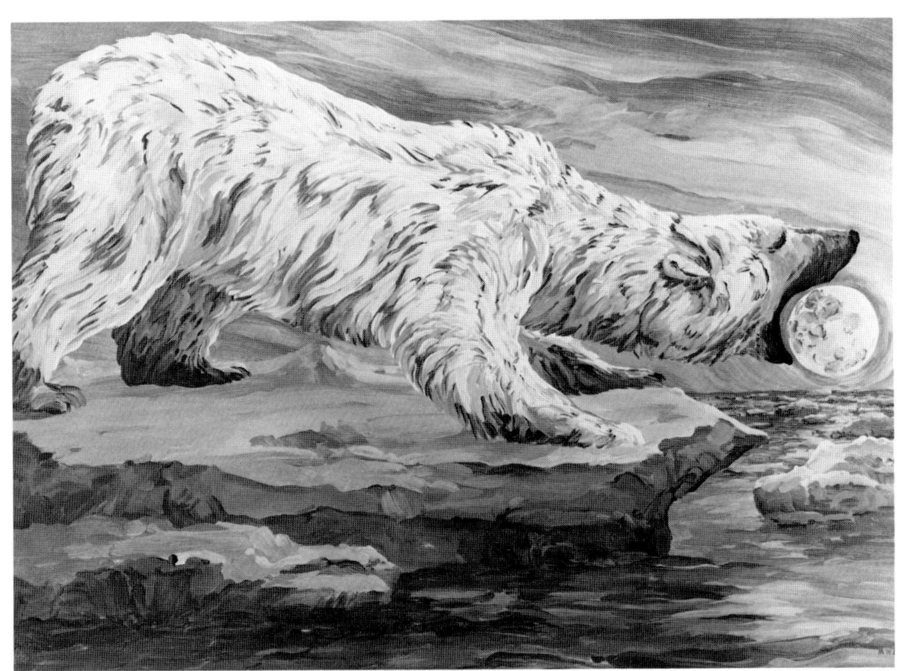

Mouthful, 1984
acrylic on paper
22 x 30″
Collection Mr. and Mrs. Martin Gutner

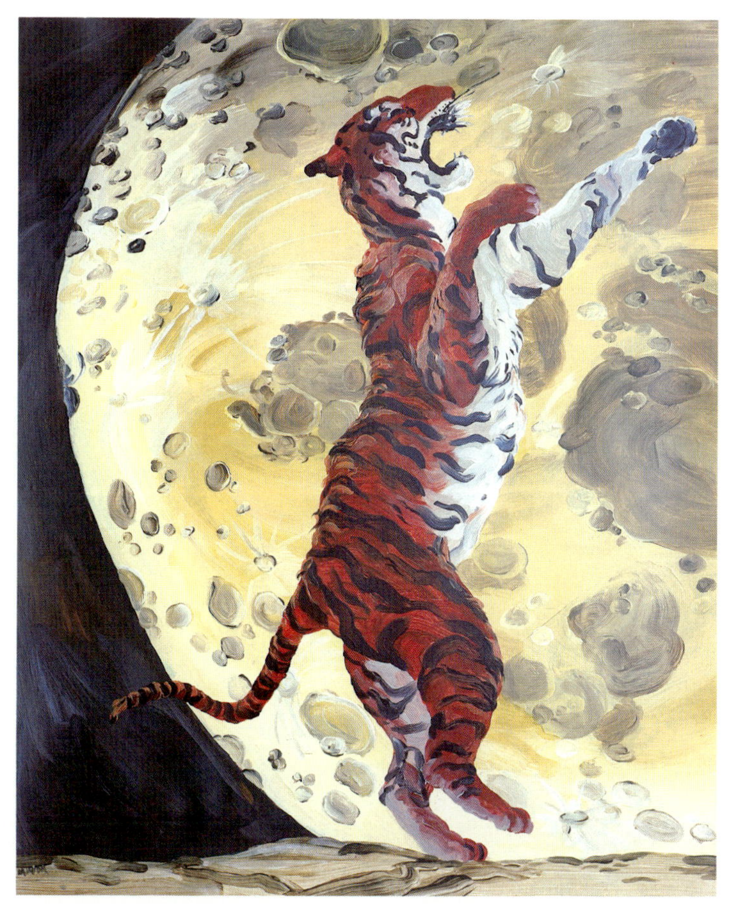

Moon, 1983
acrylic on paper
29 x 23″
Collection Paul F. Walter

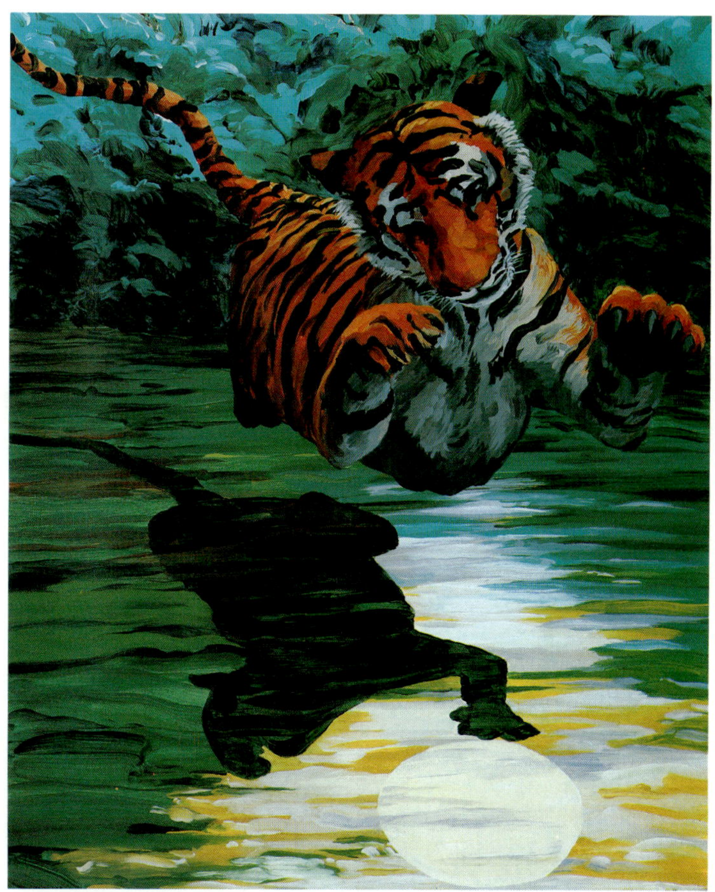

Reflection, 1984
acrylic on paper
29 x 23″
Collection Mrs. Phyllis Teplitz

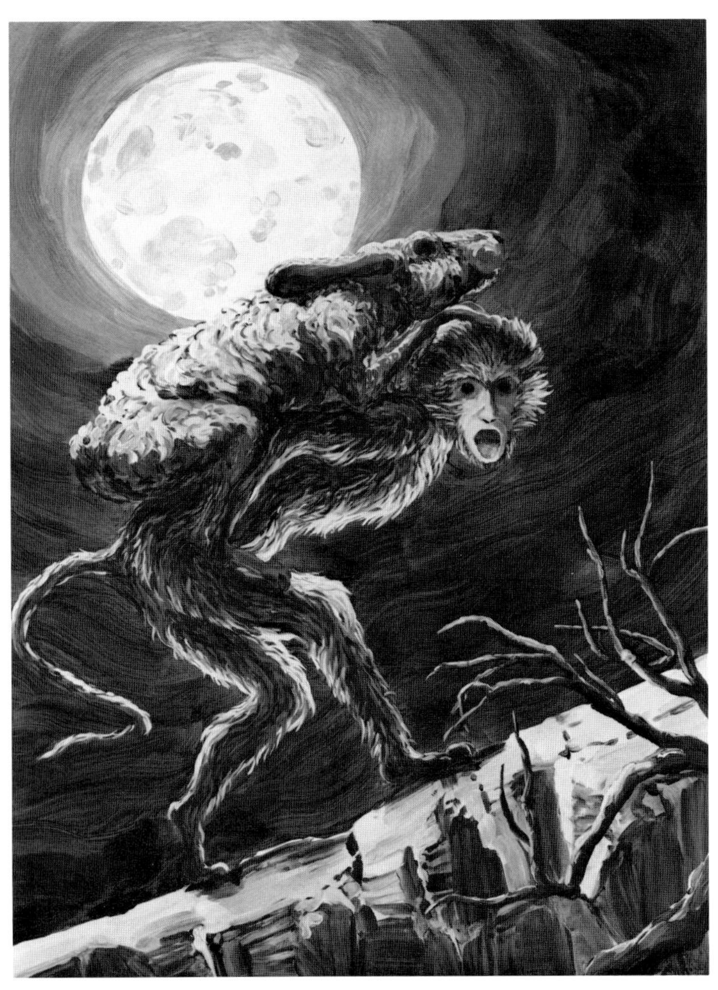

Piggyback, 1984
acrylic on paper
30 x 22″
Collection Mr. and Mrs. Marvin Gerstin

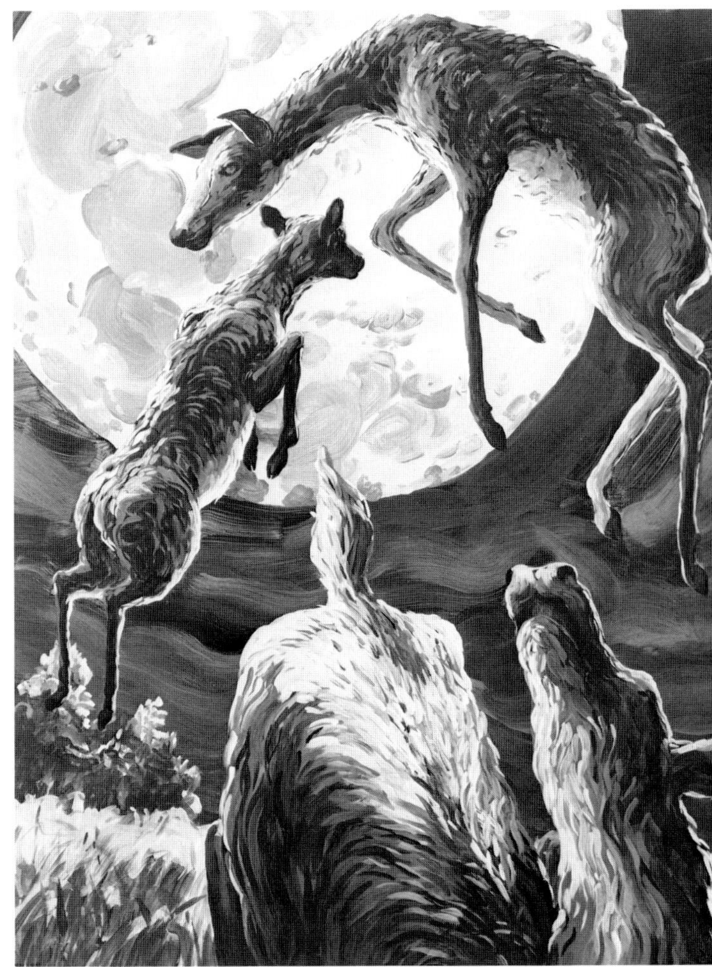

Leaping Doe, 1984
acrylic on paper
30 x 22″
Collection The First National Bank of Chicago

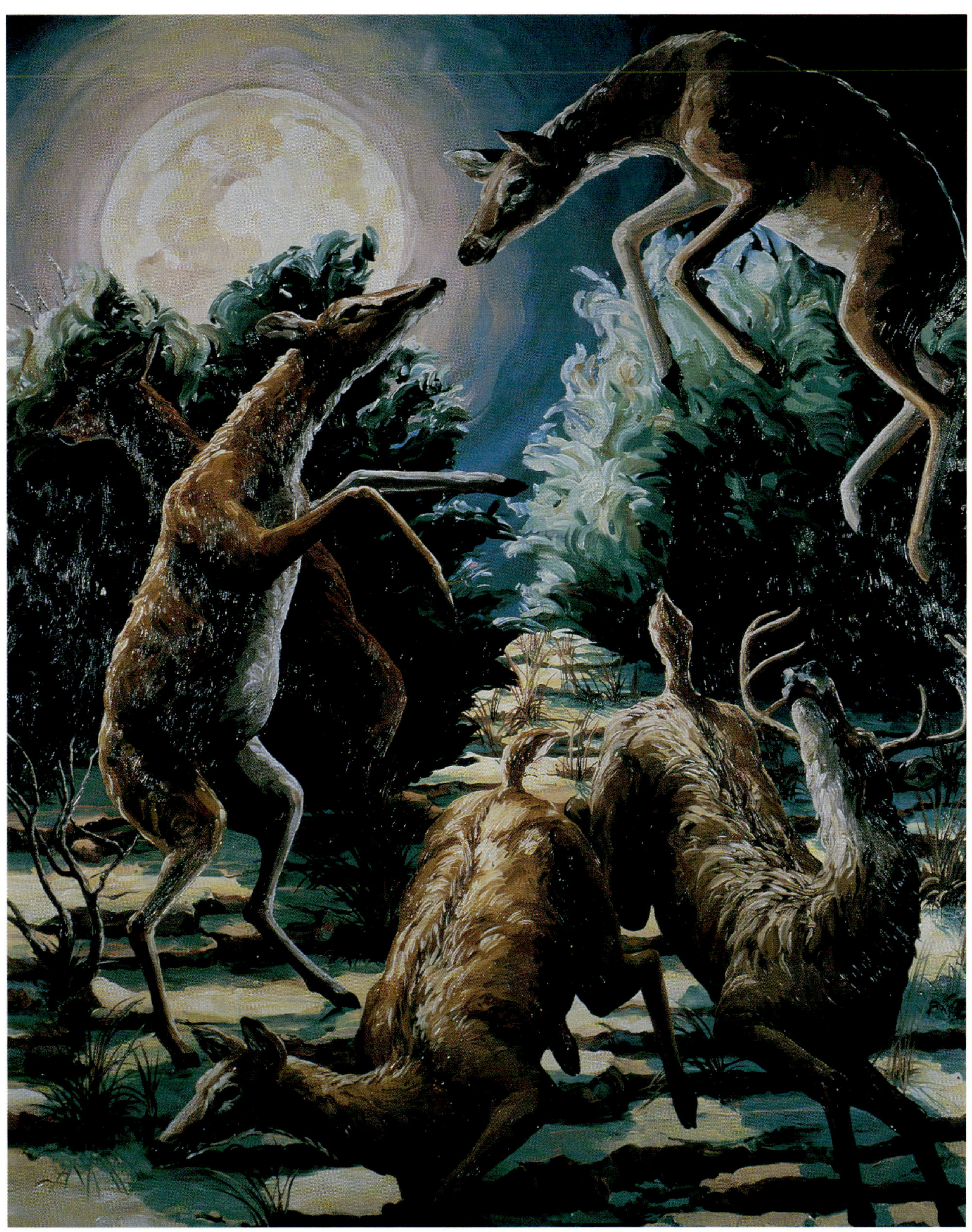

Deer Dance, 1984
oil on linen
84 x 67"
Private Collection, New York
Courtesy Holly Solomon Gallery

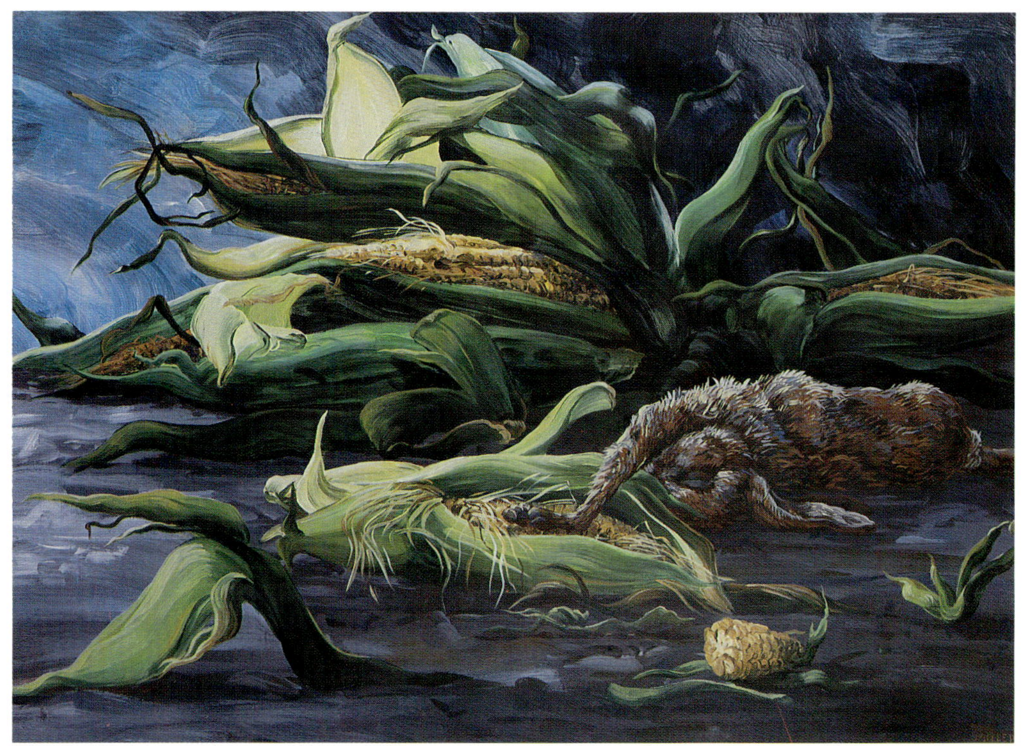

Nighteaters: Corn, 1984
acrylic on paper
22 x 30"
Collection Mr. and Mrs. Alfred H. Ebert, Houston

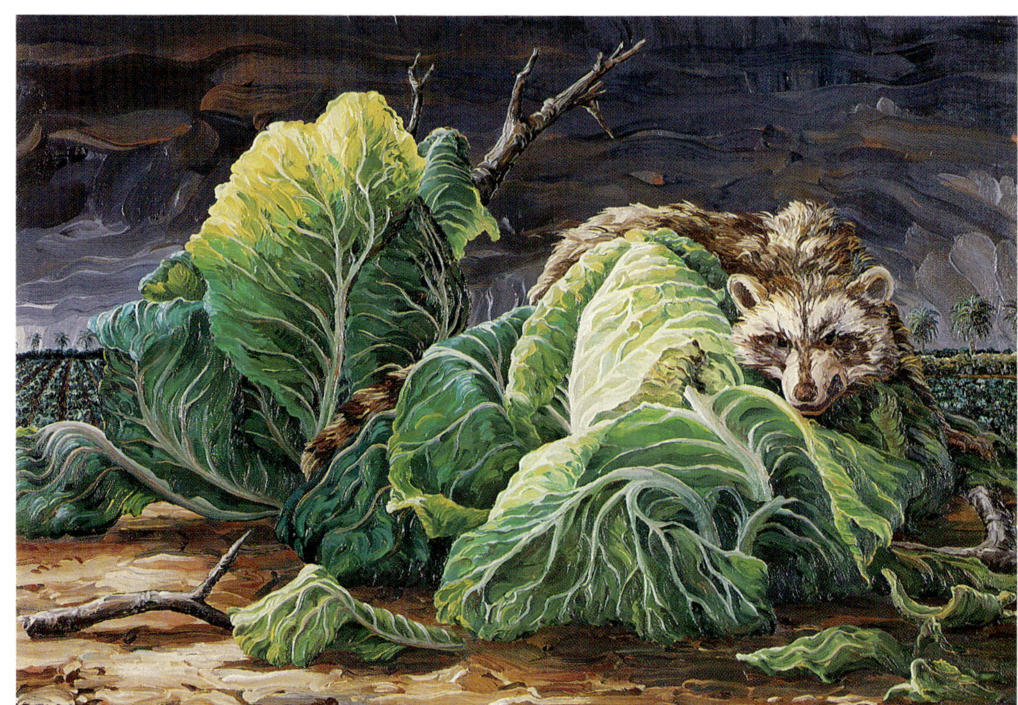

Nighteaters: Raccoon and Cabbage, 1984
oil on linen
24 x 34"
Courtesy Texas Gallery, Houston

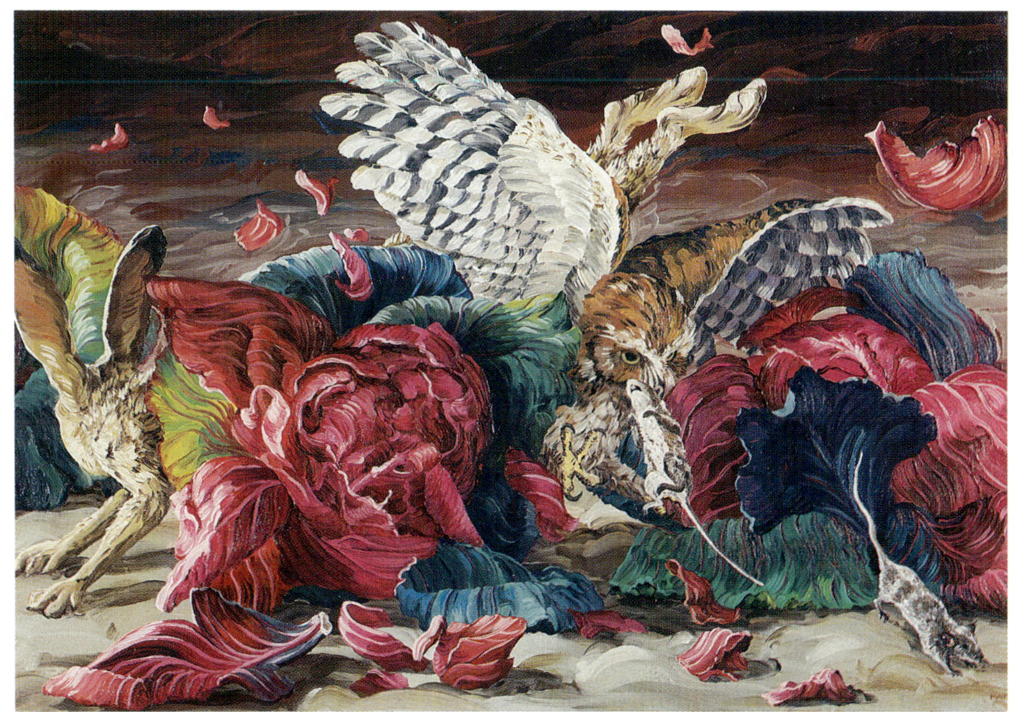

Nighteaters: Owl, 1985
oil on linen
24 x 34"
Collection the artist

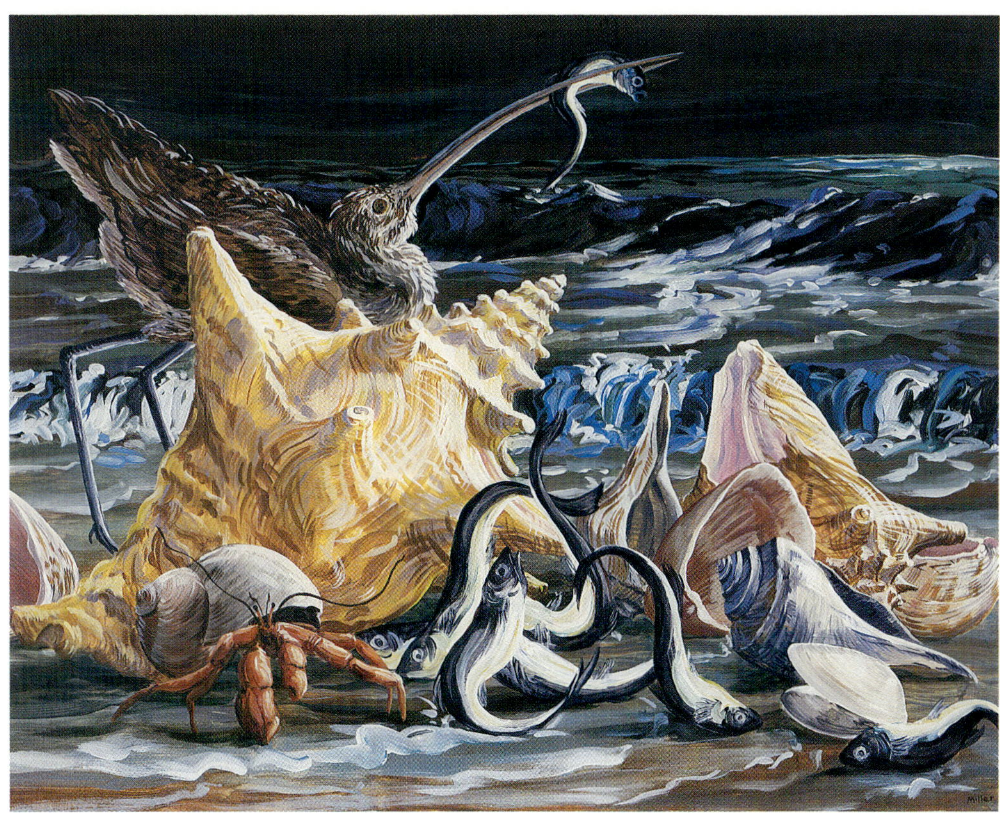

Nighteaters: Shoreline, 1985
acrylic on paper
23 x 29"
Private Collection, New York
Courtesy Holly Solomon Gallery

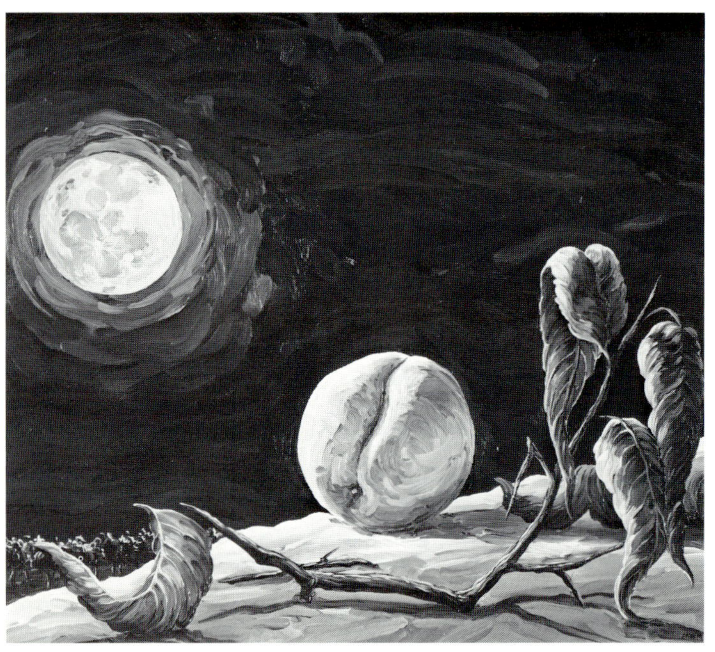

Moon and Peach, 1984
oil on linen
18 x 20"
Collection Mr. and Mrs. Ben F. Love, Houston

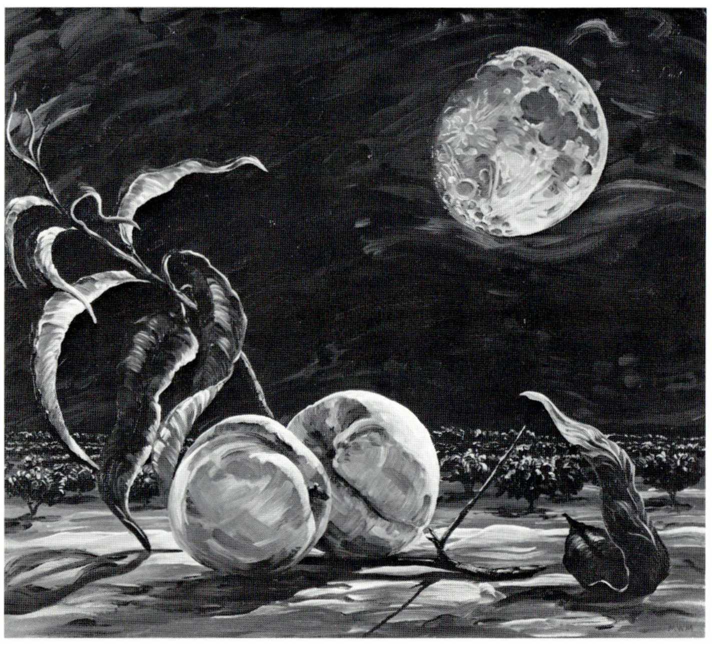

Seventh Day Moon, 1985
oil on linen
18 x 20"
Private Collection

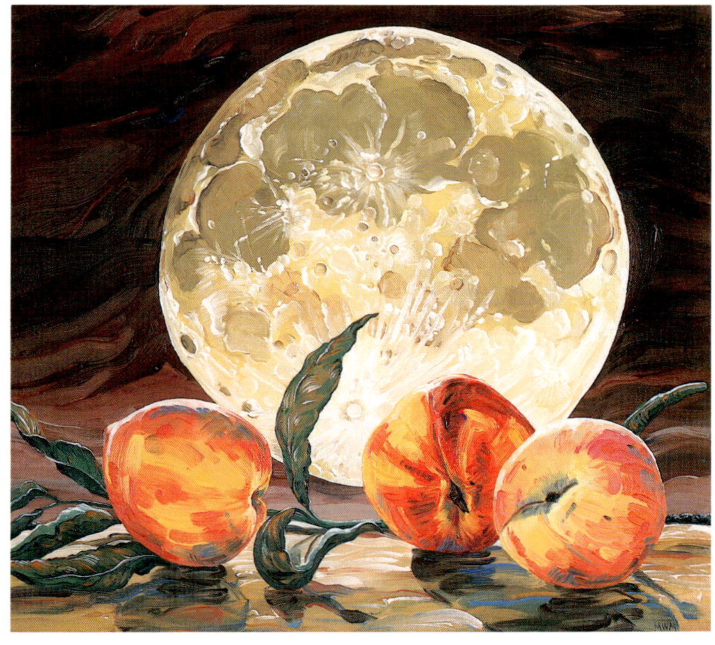

Moon Trio, 1985
oil on linen
18 x 20"
Collection Carol A. Straus

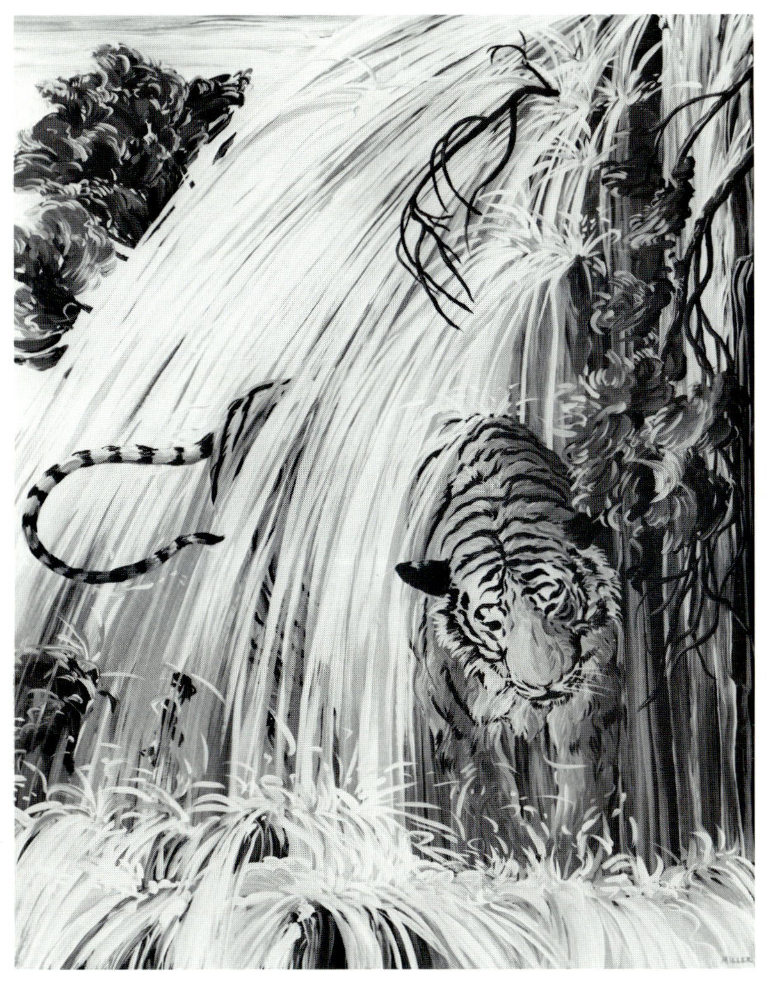

Bathing Tiger, 1984
acrylic on paper
30 x 22″
Collection John and Susie Kalil

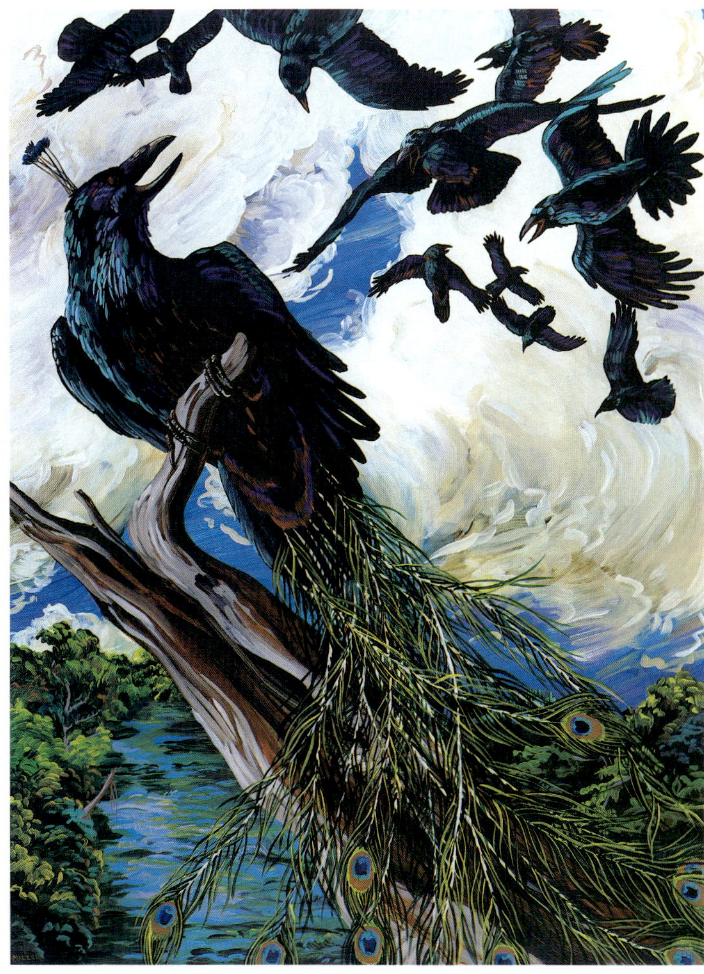

Raven as Peacock, 1985
acrylic on paper
30 x 22″
Collection Loretta and Robert K. Lifton

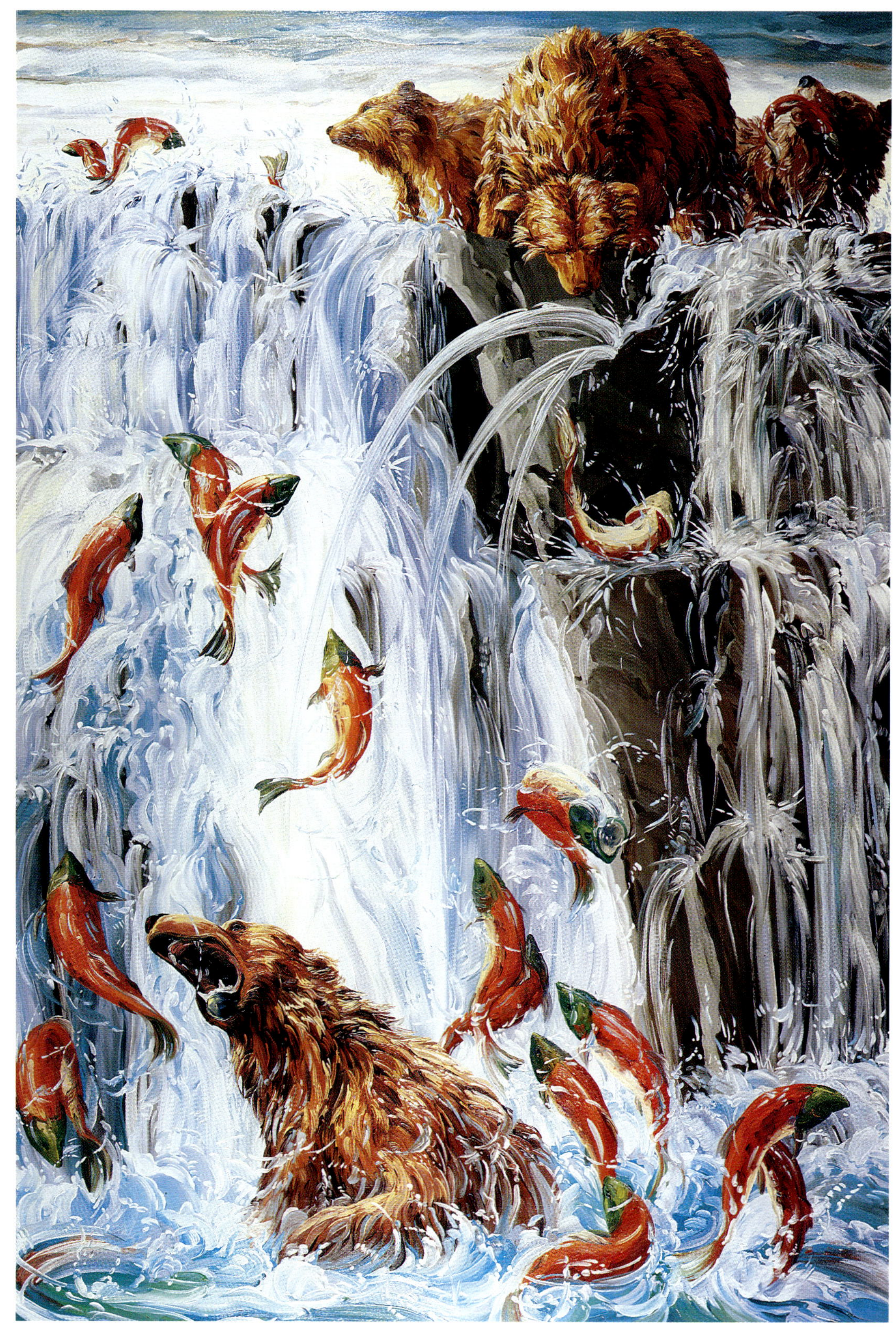

Salmon Run, 1984
oil on linen
90 x 60"
Collection Thomas and Shirley Davis

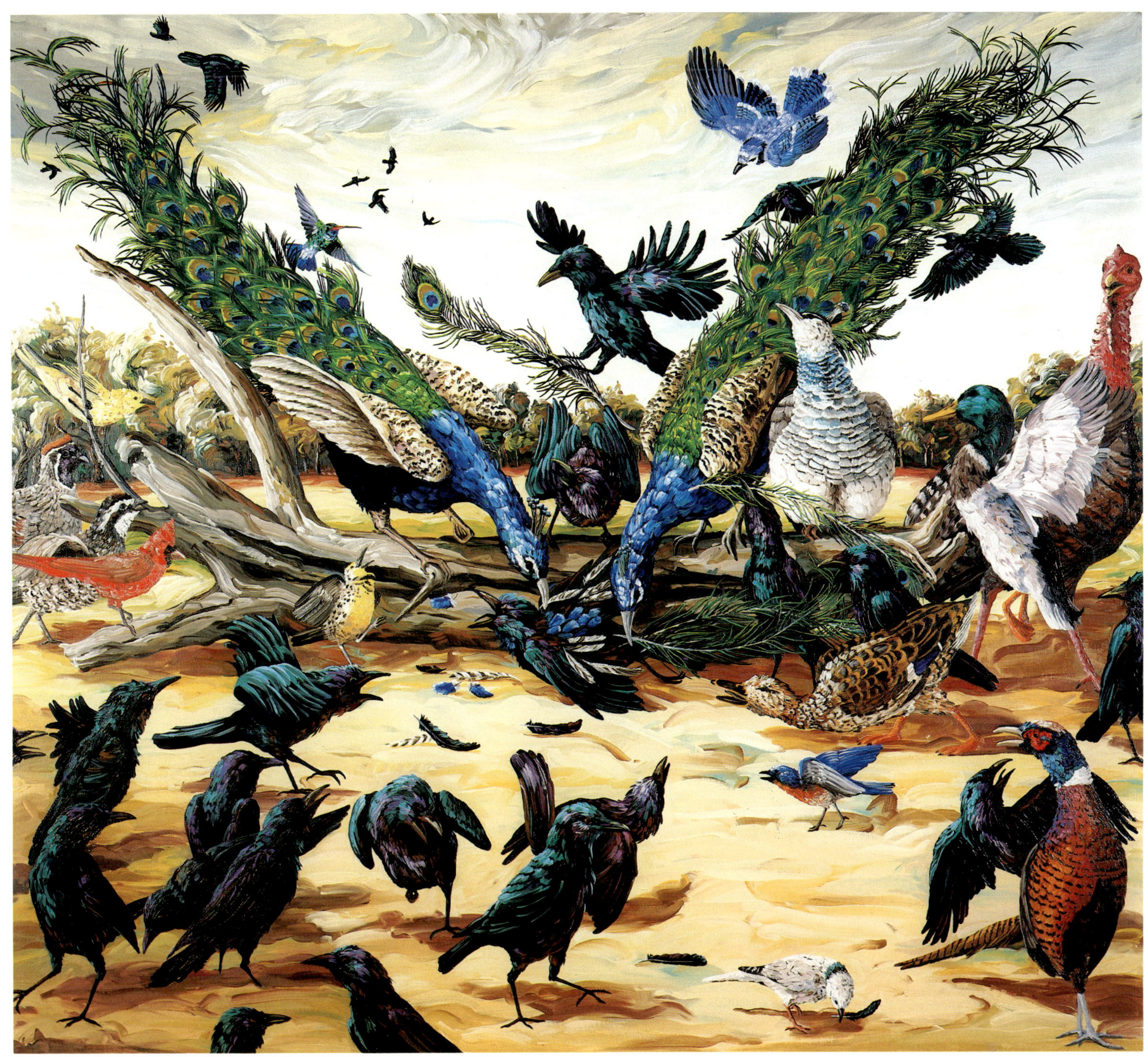

Aesop's Crow, 1985
oil on linen
66 x 72″
Promised Gift of Mr. and Mrs. Armand J. Castellani
to the Collection of the Albright-Knox Art Gallery,
Buffalo, New York

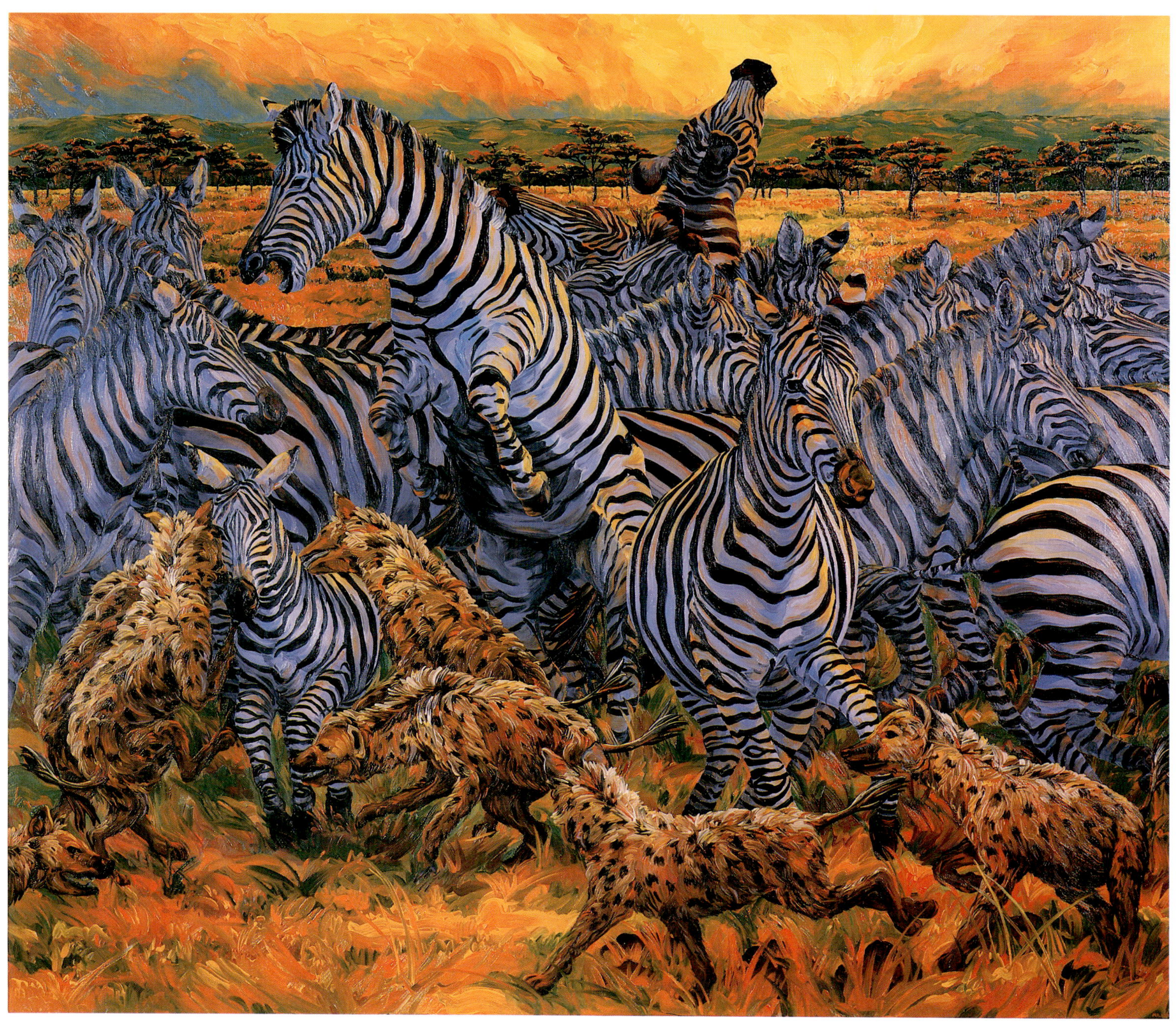

Zebras and Hyenas, 1985
oil on linen
72 x 84"
Collection Archer M. Huntington Art Gallery,
The University of Texas at Austin,
Michener Collection Acquisition Fund, 1986

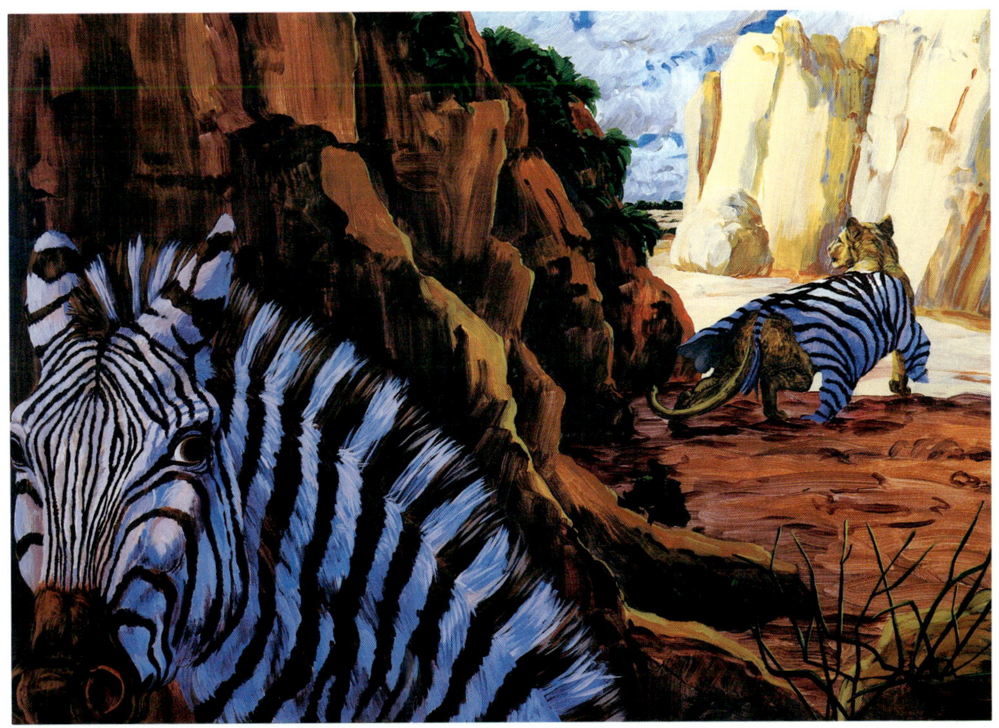

Lioness in Zebra Skin, 1985
acrylic on paper
22 x 30″
Collection Robin and Alexander Stuart

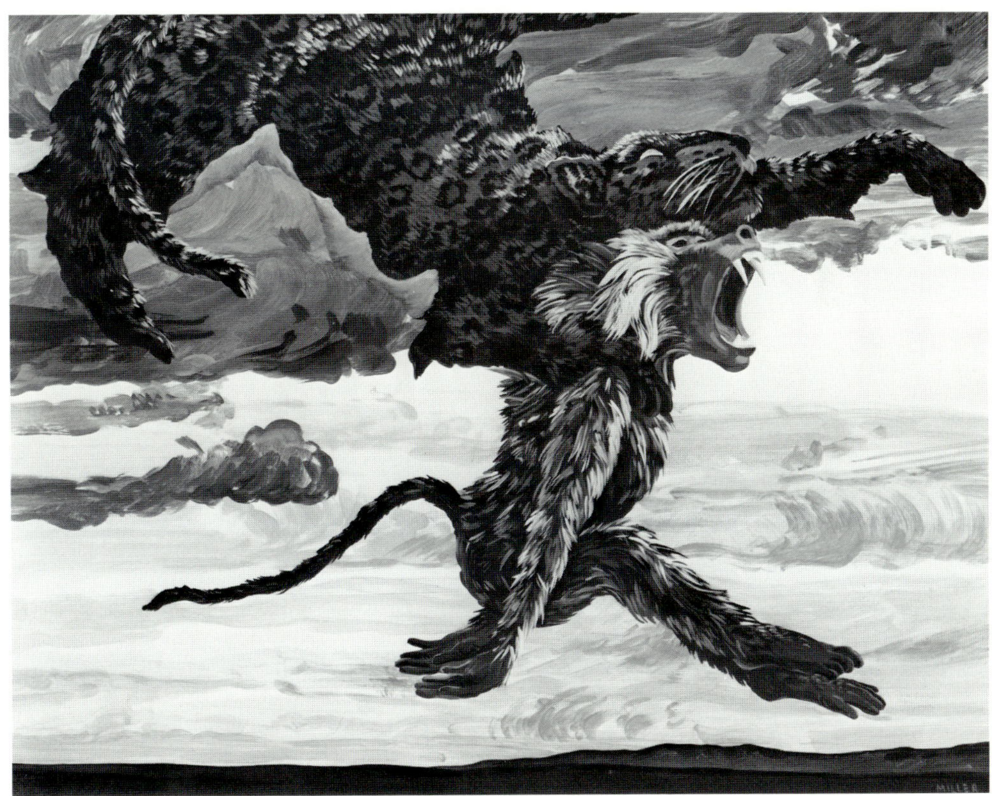

Baboon in Leopard Cape, 1985
acrylic on paper
23 x 29″
Collection Laila and Thurston Twigg-Smith

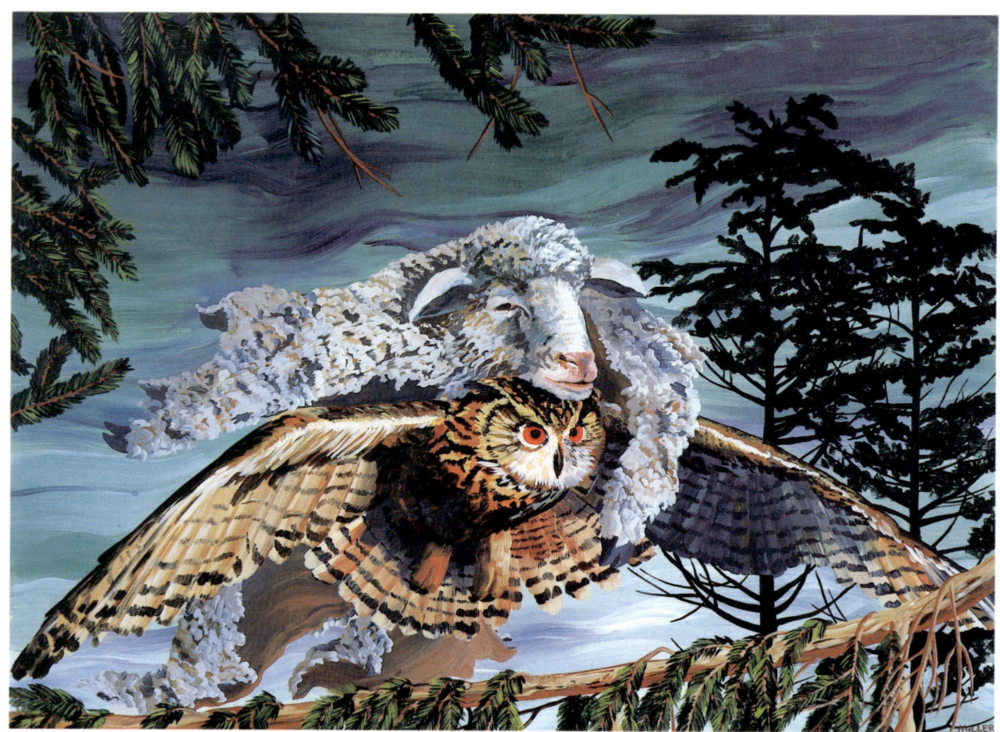

Owl in Sheep's Clothing, 1985
acrylic on paper
22 x 30"
Collection Mr. and Mrs. Sanford W. Criner Jr.

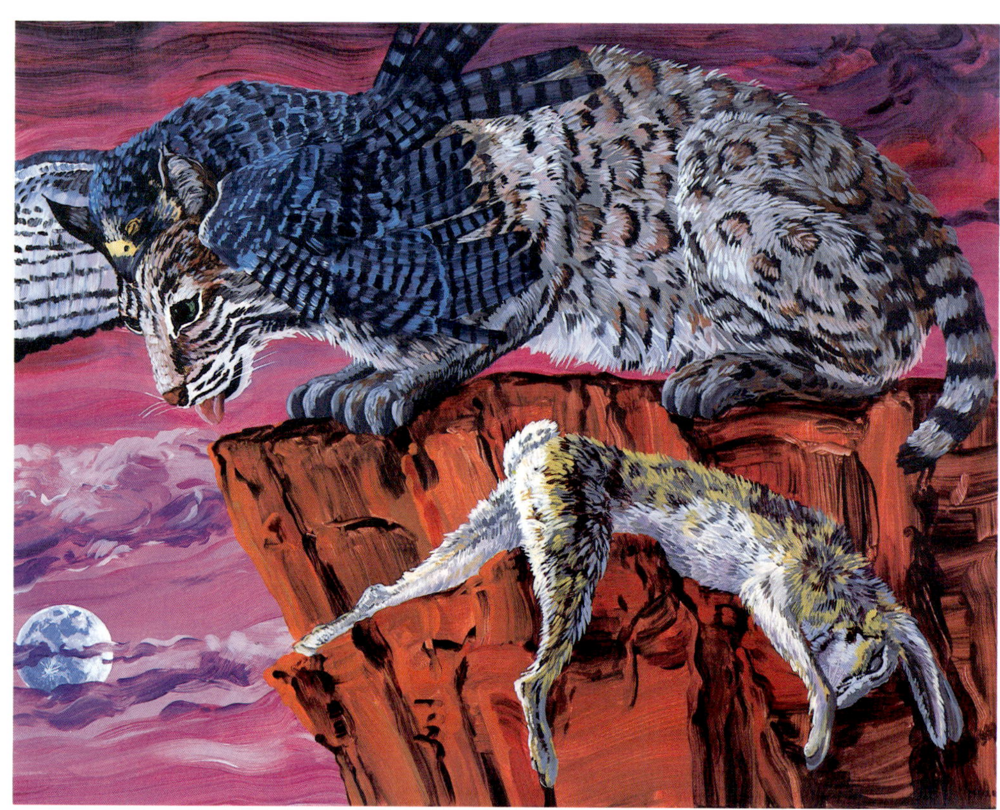

Bobcat with Falconhead, 1985
acrylic on paper
23 x 29"
Collection Mike Chesser, Los Angeles

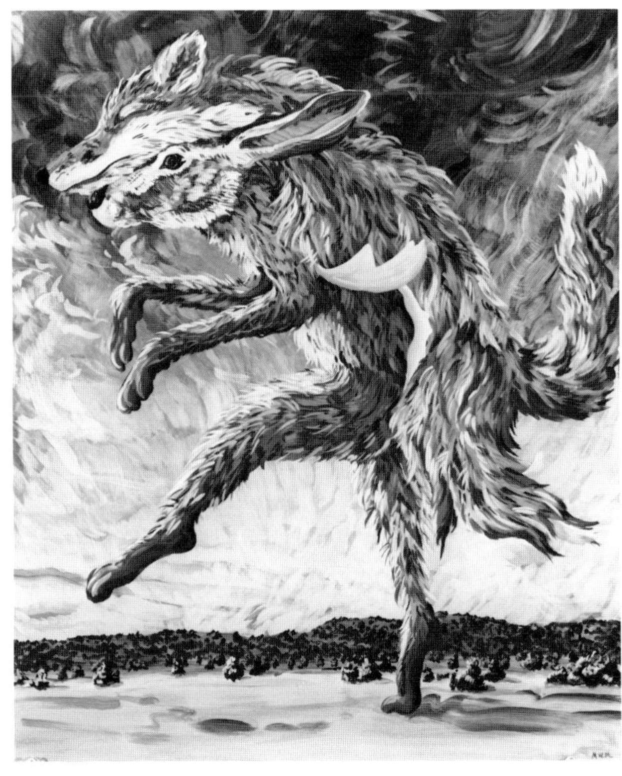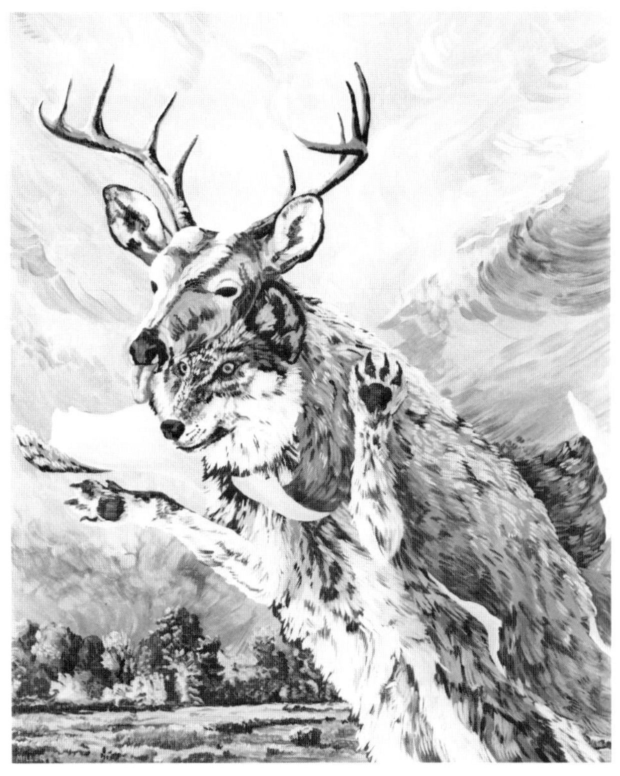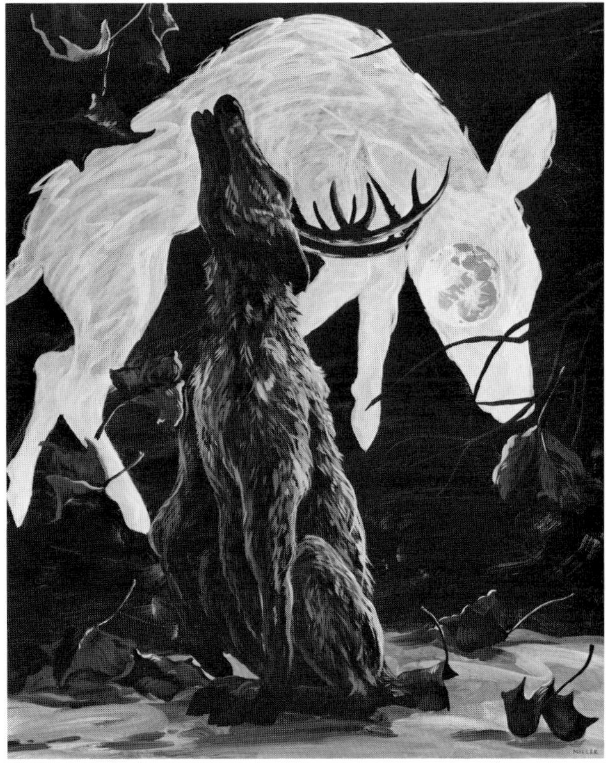

Rabbit Parading as a Fox, 1985
acrylic on paper
29 x 23″
Collection Thomas H. and Suzanne B. Dungan

Wolf Dancing as Deer, 1985
acrylic on paper
29 x 23″
Collection Mr. and Mrs. S. Patrick Woodson III

Deer Spirit, 1986
acrylic on paper
29 x 23″
Collection Mr. and Mrs. Edward R. Hudson Jr.

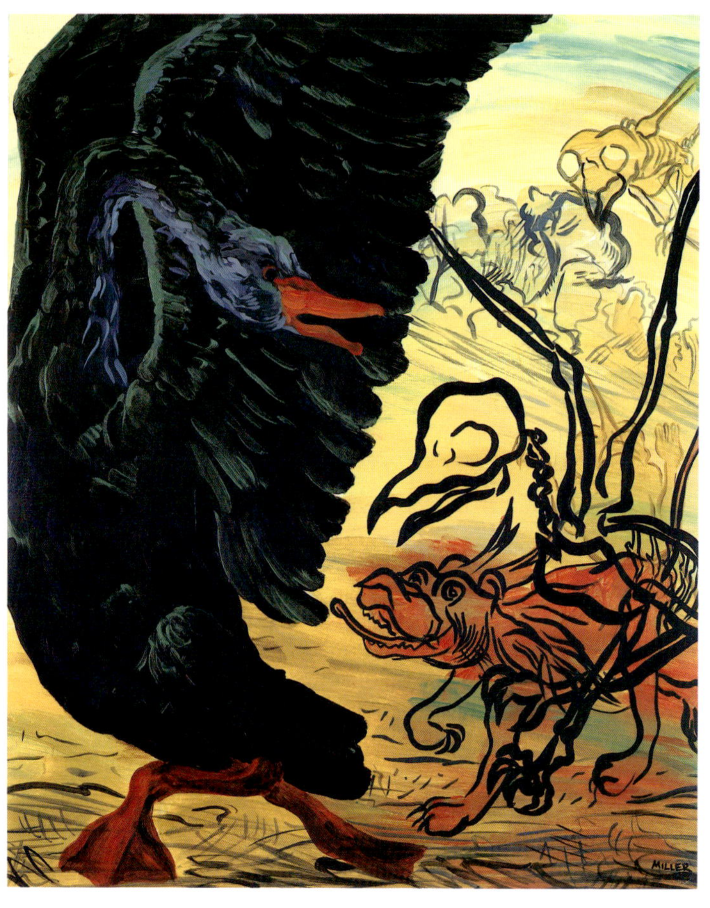

Flight from Demons, 1986
acrylic on paper
29 x 23″
Courtesy Texas Gallery, Houston

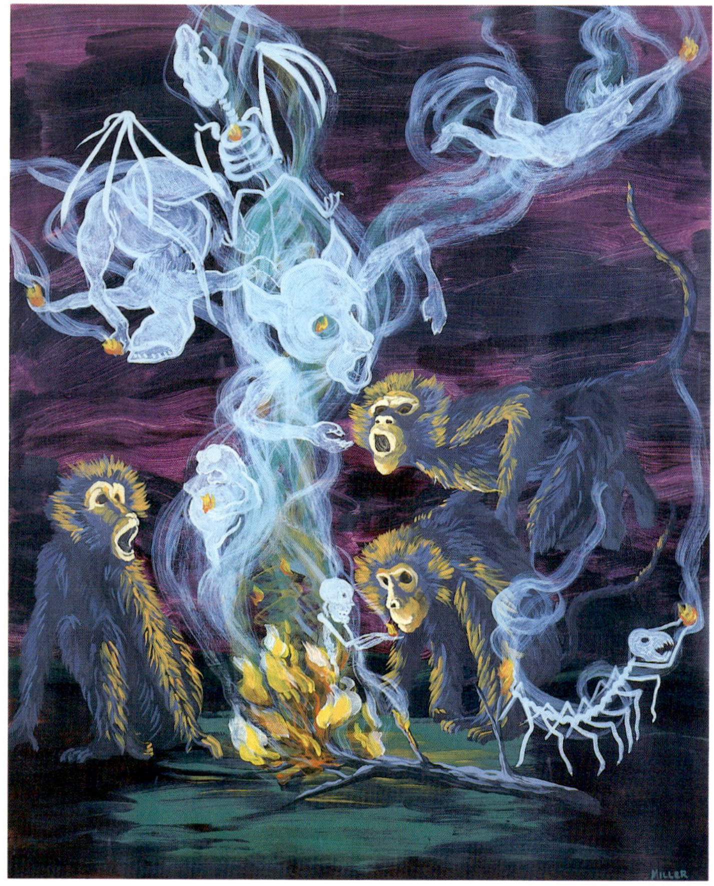

Smoky Spirits, 1986
acrylic on paper
29 x 23″
Collection Mr. and Mrs. Fred M. Halpern

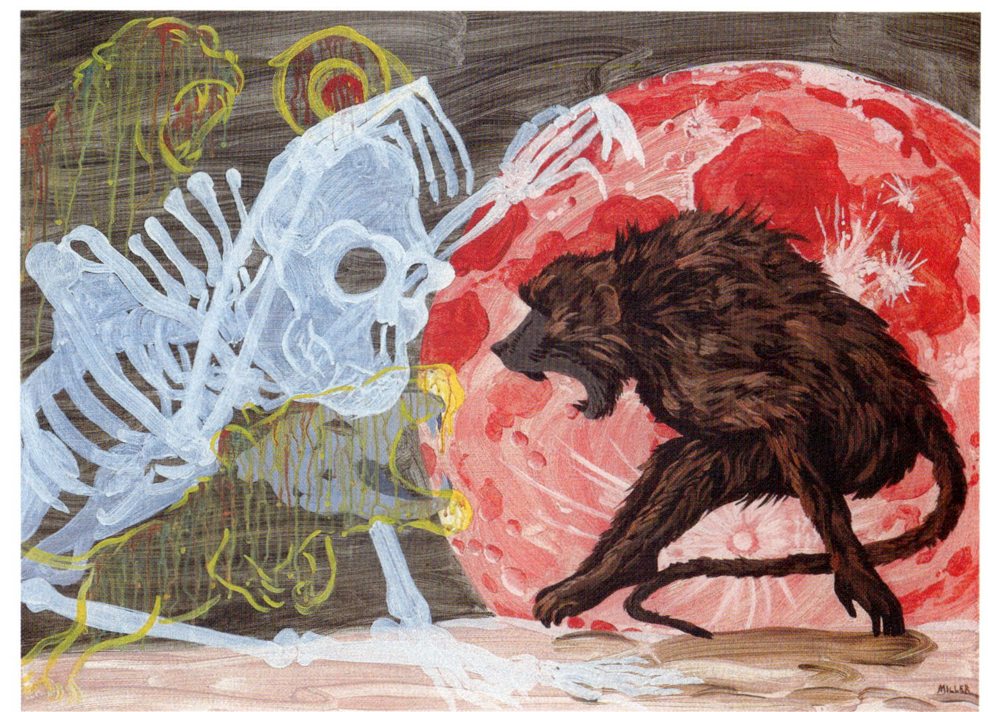

Confronting Demons, 1986
acrylic on paper
22 x 30″
Private Collection

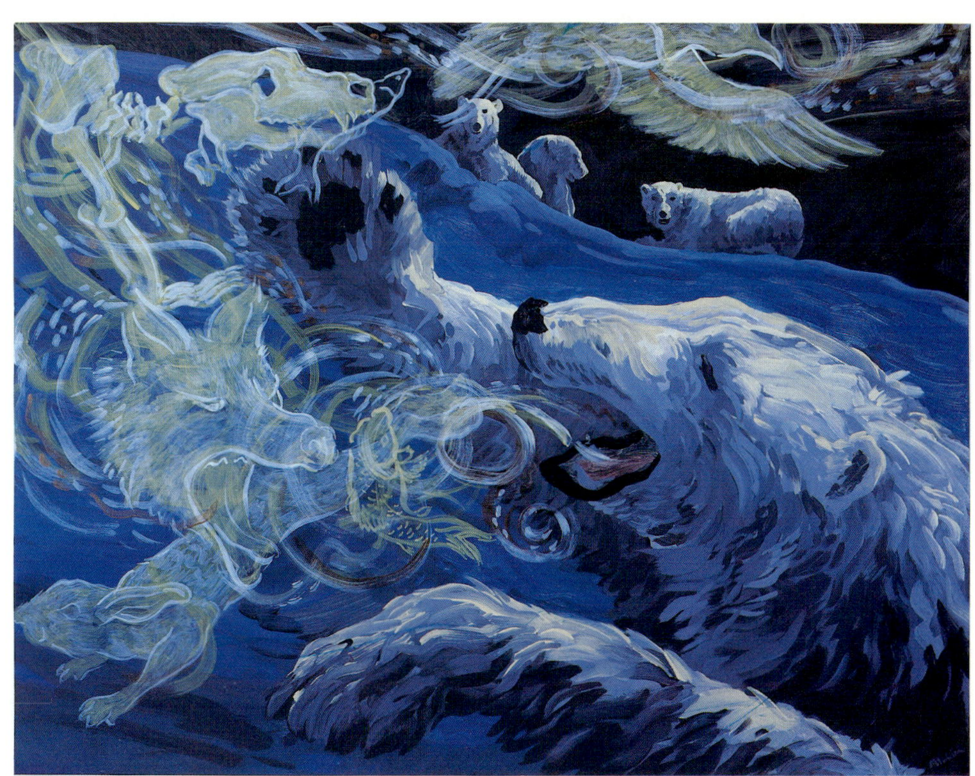

Exhale, 1986
acrylic on paper
23 x 29″
Private Collection, Houston

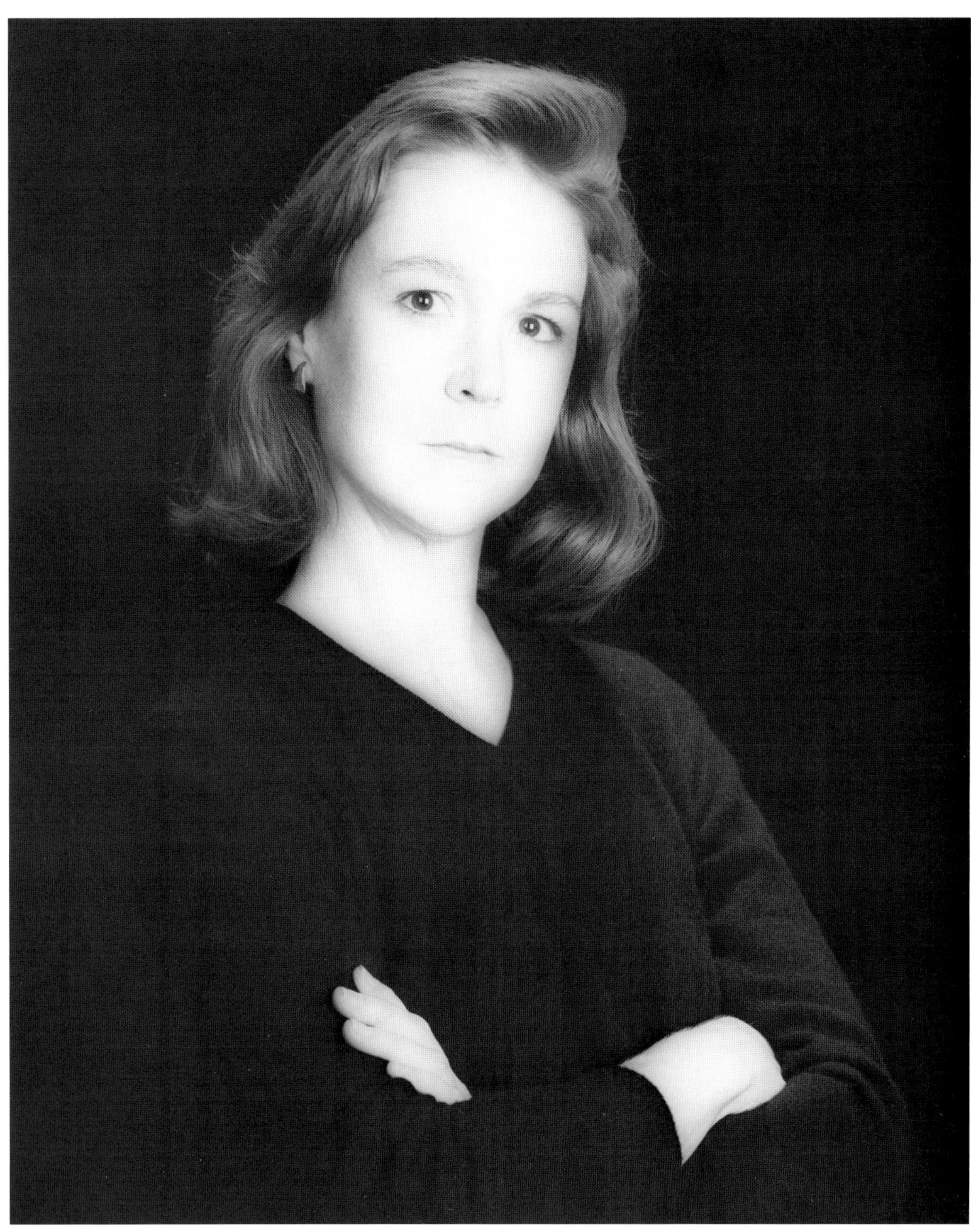

Portrait of the artist by Robert Mapplethorpe, 1986

Melissa Wren Miller was born in Houston, Texas on March 3, 1951. Between 1969 and 1972, she attended The University of Texas at Austin to study Fine Arts. In the fall of 1971, she went to The Museum of Fine Arts School in Houston. Between 1972 and 1974, she attended The University of New Mexico, Albuquerque, and received her BFA in Drawing in 1974. In the summer of 1974, she attended Yale University Summer School of Music and Art in Norfolk, Connecticut.

Three times Miller has been given Grants to Individual Artists awards from the National Endowment for the Arts: 1979, 1982 and 1985. In 1982, she was awarded the Anne Giles Kimbrough Award from the Dallas Museum of Art.

Miller currently lives and works in Austin, Texas.

Arranged chronologically.

1978 Amarillo Art Center, Texas.
Melissa Miller: An exhibition of Paintings and Drawings,
June 28-July 30.
Catalogue, *Young Texas Artists Series,* text by Thomas A. Livesay.

"Works of 3 Women to be exhibited at Art Center." *Amarillo Sunday News-Globe* (Amarillo), June 25, 1978, sec. B, p. 16.

Daviee, Jerry M. "Reviews: Lisa Baack, Carol Ivey and Melissa Miller at the Amarillo Art Center." *Artspace* (Albuquerque), vol. 2, no. 4, Summer 1978, pp. 41, 42.

1981 Art Museum of South Texas, Corpus Christi.
Melissa Miller,
April 24-June 7.

Contemporary Arts Museum, Houston, Texas.
Melissa Miller: Recent Paintings,
December 19, 1981-January 24, 1982.
Catalogue text by Linda L. Cathcart.

Crossley, Mimi. "Art Notes." *The Houston Post* (Houston), December 14, 1981, sec. B, p. 12.

Johnson, Patricia C. "Miller's Paintings Show her Youth and Enthusiasm." *Houston Chronicle* (Houston), December 25, 1981, sec. 5, p. 1.

Crossley, Mimi. "Paintings by Melissa Miller." *The Houston Post* (Houston), January 1, 1982, sec. D, p. 6.

Kalil, Susie. "Melissa Miller." *ARTnews* (New York), vol. 81, no. 5, May 1982, p. 149.

Smitherman, Leigh. "Melissa Miller." *ArtScene* (Houston), vol. 3, no. 7, Spring 1982, p. 6.

1983 Texas Gallery, Houston.
Melissa Miller,
November 8-December 3.

Kalil, Susie. "Paintings by Zakanitch, Miller, Harris and Kline." *The Houston Post* (Houston), November 20, 1983, sec. F, p. 8.

Johnson, Patricia C. "Austin artist Melissa Miller is a fast-rising star." *Houston Chronicle* (Houston), November 24, 1983, sec. 2, p. 9.

Kalil, Susie. "Reviews, Houston: Melissa Miller at Texas Gallery." *Art in America* (New York), vol. 72, no. 4, April 1984, pp. 192-194.

Hauser, Reine. "Reviews, Houston: Melissa Miller." *ARTnews* (New York), vol. 83, no. 5, May 1984, pp. 131, 134.

Exhibitions and Reviews
One-Artist Exhibitions

1984 Holly Solomon Gallery, New York.
Melissa Miller: New Work,
April 27-May 28.

Brenson, Michael. "Kim MacConnel and Melissa Miller." *The New York Times* (New York), May 11, 1984, sec. C, p. 25.

O'Brien, Glenn. "Melissa Miller, Holly Solomon Gallery." *Artforum* (New York), vol. 23, no. 2, October 1984, pp. 91, 92.

1985 Texas Gallery, Houston.
Melissa Miller,
October 1-25.

Everingham, Carol J. "Texas artist exhibits drama through classicism." *The Houston Post* (Houston), October 12, 1985, sec. G, p. 3.

Johnson, Patricia C. "Miller's work now showing greater range." *Houston Chronicle* (Houston), October 19, 1985, sec. 4, pp. 1, 7.

Broadwater, Lisa. "Editor's Notebook: Art Notes." *Texas Homes* (Dallas), vol. 9, no. 10, October 1985, pp. 9, 10.

Everingham, Carol J. "Houston Letter." *Artspace* (Albuquerque), vol. 10, no. 1, Winter 1985-86, pp. 55, 56.

Holly Solomon Gallery, New York.
Melissa Miller,
November 7-30.

Wolff, Theodore F. "Original voices in art." *The Christian Science Monitor* (Boston), November 25, 1985, Arts-Leisure section, pp. 35, 40.

Levin, Kim. "Melissa Miller." *The Village Voice* (New York), vol. 30, no. 48, November 26, 1985, p. 74.

Larson, Kay. "Pure in Spirit." *New York Magazine* (New York), vol. 18, no. 48, December 2, 1985, p. 148.

Gill, Susan. "New York Reviews: Melissa Miller." *ARTnews* (New York), vol. 85, no. 1, January 1986, p. 129.

1973   Fine Arts Center, University of New Mexico, Albuquerque.
Mid-America College Art Association Conference Special Exhibition,
Summer.

A.S.A. Gallery, University of New Mexico, Albuquerque.
Wiley, Edwards, Miller, Jurkiewicz: Paintings and Drawings,
September 4-21.

1974   Museum of Fine Arts, Museum of New Mexico, Santa Fe.
1974 Southwest Fine Arts Biennial,
May 26-August 27.
Catalogue introduction by D. O. Strel.

1977   Laguna Gloria Art Museum, Austin, Texas (in conjunction with Women and Their Work).
Women and Their Works,
October 14-November 27.

One Seguin Art Center, Seguin, Texas.
Painting and Sculpture Exhibition,
November 11-December 2.
Catalogue text by Karen Lynn Jeffers.

1978   Dallas Museum of Fine Arts, Texas.
Works on Paper: Southwest 1978,
October 25-November 26.
Catalogue text by Robert M. Murdock.
Traveled extensively throughout Texas, 1978-79

St. Edwards University, Austin, Texas.
Austin Contemporary Visual Arts Association Group Exhibition.

1979   Aperture Gallery, Austin, Texas (organized by Women and Their Work).
Vital Signs: An Exhibition of Visual Art,
February 14-March 14.
Traveled to the Academic Center of The University of Texas at Austin, March 16-30, 1979.

Carraro, Francine. "'Vital Signs' from Women and Their Work." *Artweek* (Oakland), vol. 10, no. 12, March 24, 1979, p. 3.

Trinity House Gallery, Austin, Texas.
Austin Contemporary Art Exhibition,
May 12-June 7.
Catalogue text by Richard Koshalek.

Amarillo Art Center, Texas.
The Amarillo Competition, 1979,
October 27-December 9.
Catalogue text by Jerry M. Daviee, juror's statement by John Canaday.

Group Exhibitions

Dougherty Cultural Arts Center, Austin, Texas (organized by Women and Their Work).
Women-In-Sight: New Art in Texas,
October 28-December 9.
Catalogue texts by Marcia Tucker and Rita Starpattern.

Platt, Susan. "Women in Sight: Issues of Quality, Quantity and Politics." *Artweek* (Oakland), vol. 10, no. 39, November 24, 1979, p. 13.

Laguna Gloria at First Federal, Austin, Texas.
New Works: Recent Works by Austin Artists: Melissa Miller and Claudia Reese,
October 29-November 9.
Brochure statement by the artist.

Bolger, Kathryn McKenna. "Exhibit makes itself felt." *Austin American-Statesman* (Austin), November 2, 1979, sec. D, p. 3.

Monte Vista Gallery, San Antonio, Texas.
Three Person Show, Special Exhibition for the American Arts Council.

1980 Longview Museum and Arts Center, Texas.
Invitational '80,
March 8-May 2.
Brochure statement by Thomas A. Livesay.

Laguna Gloria Art Museum, Austin, Texas.
Texas Fine Arts 1980 Annual National Exhibition,
May 10-June 22.
Catalogue statement by Linda L. Cathcart.
Traveled extensively in Texas, 1980-81.

Bolger, Kathryn McKenna. "'New Ideas' shake up annual TFAA exhibit at Laguna Gloria." *Austin American-Statesman* (Austin), May 18, 1980, Show World section, p. 33.

Robinson Galleries, Houston, Texas.
Introductions '80,
July 12-August 1.

Crossley, Mimi. "'Introductions '80.'" *The Houston Post* (Houston), July 22, 1980, sec. B, p. 8.

Tennant, Donna. "Introductions mixes new, established artists." *Houston Chronicle* (Houston), July 26, 1980, sec. 2, p. 7.

Kalil, Susie. "Houston Art Wave." *Artweek* (Oakland), vol. 11, no. 26, August 2, 1980, p. 15.

Laguna Gloria Art Museum, Austin, Texas.
Texas Only, Texas Fine Arts Association Summer Exhibition 1980,
August 23-September 14.
Brochure statement by Ron Gleason.

New Orleans Museum of Art, Louisiana.
1980 New Orleans Triennial,
October 4-November 16.
Catalogue text by Marcia Tucker.

Green, Roger. "Southern Artists in Spotlight." *The Times Picayune* (New Orleans), October 3, 1980, Lagniappe section, pp. 6, 7.

Bookhardt, Eric. "New Orleans Triennial." *Atlanta Art Papers* (Atlanta), vol. 4, no. 6, November/December 1980, p. 12.

The Art Gallery, California State University, Fullerton.
Visions & Figurations,
November 7-December 11.
Catalogue text by Rod Faulds and Winnefred Oak.

Ewing, Robert. "Figures and Narratives." *Artweek* (Oakland), vol. 11, no. 40, November 29, 1980, pp. 1, 6.

Kurcfeld, Michael. "Art: Visions and Figurations." *New West Magazine* (Los Angeles), December 1, 1980, p. 18.

Wilson, William. "'Eccentrics' In Exhibition at CSF." *Los Angeles Times* (Los Angeles), December 1, 1980, sec. 4, p. 7.

1981   Longview Museum and Arts Center, Texas.
Invitational '81,
March 7-April 24.
Checklist.

Singley, Elaine. "LMAC exhibit at panorama of experimental art." *Morning Journal* (Longview), March 22, 1981, sec. H, p. 3.

The Patrick Gallery, Austin, Texas.
Mysterious Messages,
March 17-April 11.

Bolger, Kathryn McKenna. "Mysterious messages lurk within paintings, sculptures." *Austin American-Statesman* (Austin), March 19, 1981, sec. B, p. 10.

Nichols, Tom. "Mystery abounds in Patrick show." *Citizen Marquee* (Austin), March 20, 1981, p. 7.

Mattingly Baker Gallery, Dallas, Texas.
Wendy Edwards and Melissa Miller,
May 16-June 18.

Berryhill, Michael. "Gallery art styles don't blend well." *Fort Worth Star-Telegram* (Fort Worth), May 31, 1981, sec. E, p. 5.

Marvel, Bill. "Gallery hopping." *Dallas Times Herald* (Dallas), June 10, 1981, sec. F, pp. 1, 7.

1982 Longview Museum and Arts Center, Texas.
Invitational '82,
March 6-April 28.
Brochure statement by David G. Turner.

Laguna Gloria Art Museum, Austin, Texas.
New Works Summer '82: Hale, Jalapeeno, Miller, Pardo, Peterson, Stanton,
July 2-25.
Catalogue introduction by Annette DiMeo Carlozzi.

Beal, Greg. "'New Works' wrap you in color." *Austin American-Statesman* (Austin), July 4, 1982, Show World section, pp. 33, 34.

Knief, Mary Kay. "New Works by Austin Artists." *Austin Homes & Gardens* (Austin), vol. 4, no. 1, July 1982, pp. 16, 17.

The Patrick Gallery, Austin, Texas.
Artists in the I-35 Corridor, Part III—Austin,
August 7-September 11.

Beal, Greg. "Patrick Gallery show falls short of its promise." *Austin American-Statesman* (Austin), August 18, 1982, sec. C, p. 1.

The University of St. Thomas Art Gallery, Houston, Texas.
Recreating the World,
November 11-December 11.
Catalogue foreword by Ann F. Bunn and Alexandra Tyson, statement by Beverly Krieger.

1983 San Antonio Art Institute, Texas.
New Figurative Drawing in Texas,
January 20-February 24.

Neal, Patsy. "Figuratives Highly Imaginative." *The San Antonio Light* (San Antonio), January 28, 1983, sec. F, p. 3.

Shown, John. "27 Talents Make One Fine Exhibit." *The Sunday Express-News* (San Antonio), January 30, 1983, sec. N, p. 6.

Archer M. Huntington Art Gallery, College of Fine Arts, University of Texas at Austin.
Images of Texas,
February 25-April 10.
Catalogue, *Texas Images and Visions,* text by William H. Goetzmann.
Traveled to Art Museum of South Texas, Corpus Christi, July 1-August 14, 1983; Amarillo Art Center, Texas, September 3-October 30, 1983.

Kutner, Janet. "Refracted 'Images'." *The Dallas Morning News* (Dallas), March 4, 1983, sec. C, pp. 1, 2.

Goetzmann, William H. "Images of Texas." *Artspace* (Albuquerque), vol. 7, no. 2, Spring 1983, pp. 20-40.

Whitney Museum of American Art, New York.
1983 Biennial Exhibition,
March 24-May 29.
Catalogue.

Russell, John. "Why the Latest Whitney Biennial Is More Satisfying." *The New York Times* (New York), March 25, 1983, sec. C, pp. 1, 26.

Sozanski, Edward J. "Annual shows: Do we really need them?" *Philadelphia Inquirer* (Philadelphia), April 10, 1983, sec. I, pp. 15, 16.

Larson, Kay. "All-American Energy." *New York Magazine* (New York), vol. 16, no. 15, April 11, 1983, pp. 61-63.

Wolff, Theodore F. "Let's not overlook the breadth of American art." *Christian Science Monitor* (Boston), April 12, 1983, p. 18.

Hoelterhoff, Manuela. "Whitney Double: No Blue Faces." *The Wall Street Journal* (New York), vol. 201, no. 74, April 15, 1983, p. 31.

Ashbery, John. "Biennials Bloom in the Spring." *Newsweek* (New York), vol. 51, no. 16, April 18, 1983, pp. 93, 94.

Levin, Kim. "Double Takes." *The Village Voice* (New York), April 26, 1983, pp. 91, 92.

Smith, Roberta. "The Whitney Biennial: Taking Consensus." *The Village Voice* (New York), April 26, 1983, pp. 91, 92.

Bassin, Joan. "Texan's Paintings look like flowers among weeds of NYC art." *Austin American-Statesman* (Austin), May 1, 1983, Show World section, pp. 58, 59.

Heartney, Eleanor. "Pessimism prevails over humanism in Whitney Biennial." *New Art Examiner* (Chicago), vol. 10, no. 8, May 1983, pp. 11, 35.

Cameron, Daniel. "Biennial Cycle." *Arts Magazine* (New York), vol. 57, no. 10, June 1983, pp. 64-68.

Cone, Michèle. "The Whitney Biennial." *Flash Art* (Milan), no. 113, Summer 1983, p. 62.

Contemporary Arts Museum, Houston, Texas.
Southern Fictions,
August 2-September 4.
Catalogue texts by William A. Fagaly and Monroe K. Spears.

Johnson, Patricia C. "The tangible enigma of the South." *Houston Chronicle* (Houston), August 7, 1983, Zest section, p. 13.

Kalil, Susie. "Southern Fictions." *The Houston Post* (Houston), August 7, 1983, sec. F, pp. 1, 7.

Fox, Kevin. "Southern Fictions." *Dallas Downtown News* (Dallas), vol. 6, no. 40, August 8-14, 1983, p. 17.

Kutner, Janet. "In the Southern tradition." *The Dallas Morning News* (Dallas), August 26, 1983, sec. C, pp. 1, 3.

Bassin, Joan. "Art of the South." *Austin American-Statesman* (Austin), August 28, 1983, Show World section, p. 37.

University Art Museum, Universtity of New Mexico, Albuquerque.
Certain Realities,
September 24-November 27.
Catalogue text by Emily Kass.

Traugott, Joseph. "Exhibit's Power Is to Shock." *Albuquerque Journal* (Albuquerque), October 16, 1983, sec. D, p. 2.

Shields, Kathleen. "Certain Realities." *Artspace* (Albuquerque), vol. 8, no. 1, Winter 1983-84, pp. 12-16.

Bell Gallery, List Art Center, Brown University, Providence, Rhode Island.
Painting: Gregory Amenoff, Howard Hodgkin, Melissa Miller, Katherine Porter, Joan Thorne, Susan Whyne,
December 3-December 30.
Catalogue introduction by Susan Finnin Yeh.

Gray, Channing. "Bold works by first-rate artists typify new direction in American painting." *The Providence Journal* (Providence), December 11, 1983, sec. H. pp. 1, 8.

"Review of Six Painters." *Newport; This Week* (Newport), December 15, 1983, pp. 17, 30.

Van Siclen, Bill. "Season's Paintings." *The New Paper* (Providence), December 21-29, 1983, sec. 1, pp. 6, 7.

Collins, Roy. "Some Exceptions to otherwise 'trendy' exhibit." *East Side Monthly* (Providence), vol. 10, no. 4, December 1983, p. 11.

The New Museum of Contemporary Art, New York.
The End of the World: Contemporary Visions of the Apocalypse,
December 10, 1983-January 22, 1984.
Catalogue text by Lynn Gumpert.

Levin, Kim. "The Day Before." *The Village Voice* (New York), vol. 29, January 3, 1984, p. 74.

Minnucci, Marilena. "Visualizing the End of the World." *The Villager* (New York), January 12, 1984, pp. 9, 10.

Glueck, Grace. "When Artists Portray Utopia and Armageddon." *The New York Times* (New York), January 15, 1984, sec. 2, pp. 33, 35.

Wolff, Theodore F. "World disaster viewed through the artist's brush." *The Christian Science Monitor* (Boston), January 16, 1984, Arts-Leisure section, p. 21.

Heartney, Eleanor. "The End of the World." *Arts Magazine* (New York), vol. 58, no. 6, February 1984, pp. 100, 101.

1984 Archer M. Huntington Art Gallery, College of Fine Arts, University of Texas at Austin.
New American Painting: A Tribute to James and Mari Michener,
January 12-March 5.
Catalogue text by Eric McCready and Becky Duval Reese.

Derrickson, Steve. "New American Painting: The Good, the Bad and the Merely Mediocre." *Austin Chronicle* (Austin), vol. 3, no. 12, February 10, 1984, p. 5.

Carraro, Francine. "Many hues of painting shine in far-reaching UT exhibit." *Austin American-Statesman* (Austin), February 12, 1984, Show World section, p. 34.

Kutner, Janet. "UT collection proves uneven." *The Dallas Morning News* (Dallas), February 23, 1984, sec. F, pp. 1, 2.

Artrain: Austin, Temple, Corsicana, Plano, Lubbock, Midland-Odessa Airport, El Paso, Longview, Texarkana, Bryan, Galveston, Texas.
Texas on My Mind: Contemporary Visions of the Lone Star State,
September 6-November 28.
Catalogue.

Reinhold, Robert. "Train Takes Art and Artists to Towns Over Texas." *The New York Times* (New York), November 8, 1984, sec. 1, p. 12.

UTSA Art Teaching Gallery, University of Texas at San Antonio.
Five Texans in Venice,
February 6-24.

Solon, Marcia. "A challenging art exhibit." *The San Antonio Light* (San Antonio), February 19, 1984, p. 31.

Donley, Ray. "Austin to Venice." *Third Coast* (Austin), vol. 3, no. 7, February 1984, pp. 83, 85.

Ennis, Michael. "Venetian Finds." *Texas Monthly* (Austin), vol. 12, no. 2, February 1984, pp. 128-133.

White Columns Gallery, New York.
Bunnies,
March 27-April 17.

McCormick, Carlo. "Bunnies." *New York Beat* (New York), April 11, 1984, p. 14.

Gallery 400, The University of Illinois, Chicago.
Four Texas Painters,
May 2-26.

1984 United States Pavilion, La 41 Biennale, Venice, Italy.
Paradise Lost/Paradise Regained: American Visions of the New Decade,
June 10-September 30.
U.S. catalogue text by Marcia Tucker.
General catalogue, *Arte e Arti: Attualita e Storia,* text by Maurizio Calvesi.
Traveled to Calouste Gulbenkian Foundation, Lisbon, Portugal, October 30-December 10;
Exhibition Hall "Pablo Ruiz Picasso," Madrid, Spain, January 10-February 25, 1985; Municipal
Art Gallery, Athens, Greece, March 10-April 30, 1985; King Stephen Museum, Budapest,
Hungary, May 15-June 30, 1985; State Painting and Sculpture Museum, Ankara, Turkey,
November 10-December 15, 1985.

Hughes, Robert. "Gliding over a Dying Reef." *Time Magazine* (New York), vol. 124, no. 1, July 2, 1984, pp. 76-78.

Hoelterhoff, Manuela. "The Venice Biennale: No Paradise for Art." *The Wall Street Journal* (New York), vol. 204, no. 21, July 31, 1984, p. 30.

Kutner, Janet. "No 'Paradise' Found." *Dallas Morning News* (Dallas), August 14, 1984, sec. E, pp. 2, 3.

Art Barn Gallery, Ellen Battell Steckel Estate, Norfolk, Connecticut.
10 Years Later: An Exhibition of Yale-Norfolk Alumni and Faculty,
June 16-June 22.

The San Francisco Museum of Modern Art, California.
The Human Condition: SFMMA Biennial III,
June 28-August 26.
Catalogue texts by Henry T. Hopkins, Dorothy Martinson, Wolfgang Max Faust, Achille Bonito
Oliva, Klaus Ottman and Edward Kienholz.

Burkhart, Dorothy. "Artists hold bleak view of 'The Human Condition'." *San José Mercury News* (San José), July 6, 1984, sec. D, pp. 1, 3.

Geeting, Karen H. "Museum Notebook: The Human Condition: SFMMA Biennial III."
Southwest Art (Houston), vol. 14, no. 3, August 1984, p. 86.

Museo Rufino Tamayo, Mexico City.
El Arte Narrativo,
November 6, 1984-January 6, 1985.
Catalogue text by Bruce Kurtz.

1985   The Museum of Fine Arts, Houston, Texas.
Fresh Paint: The Houston School,
January 26-April 7.
Catalogue texts by Susie Kalil and Barbara Rose.
Traveled to The Institute for Art and Urban Resources, Inc., P.S. 1, Long Island City,
New York, May 5-June 21, 1985; The Oklahoma Art Center, Oklahoma City, July 19-
August 11, 1985.

Everingham, Carol J. "'Fresh Paint': It's the Talk of the Town." *The Houston Post* (Houston),
January 20, 1985, sec. F, p. 1.

Holmes, Ann. "Fresh Paint." *Houston Chronicle* (Houston), January 20, 1985, Supplement
Section.

McCombie, Mel. "Art World Colors 'Fresh Paint' show in optimistic hues." *Austin American-
Statesman* (Austin), February 3, 1985, Show World section, pp. 38, 39.

Ennis, Michael. "Persistent Vigor." *Texas Monthly* (Austin), vol. 13, no. 3, March 1985, pp. 152,
153, 155-158.

McEvilley, Thomas. "Double Vision in Space City." *Artforum* (New York), vol. 23, no. 8,
April 1985, pp. 52-56.

Glueck, Grace. "A 'Houston School' Emerges for Southwest." *The New York Times* (New York),
May 25, 1985, sec. C, p. 20.

Hauser, Reine. "Reviews: Houston." *ARTnews* (New York), vol. 84, no. 6, Summer 1985,
pp. 103, 104.

San Antonio Museum of Art, Texas.
Private Treasures-Public View,
February 3-March 17.

Goddard, Dan R. "SAMA Displays Private Treasures." *Express-News* (San Antonio),
February 10, 1985, sec. H, pp. 1, 2.

The Bruce Museum, Greenwich, Connecticut.
Women of the American West,
May 19-August 31.
Catalogue text by Dorothy M. Kosinski.

"'Women of the American West' to be Exhibited at Bruce Museum." *Greenwich Times* (Greenwich), May 15, 1985, sec. A, p. 6.

"'Women of the American West' revealed at Bruce Museum." *Greenwich News* (Greenwich), May 23, 1985, sec. 2, p. 4.

Zimmer, William. "A Bit of the Old West in Greenwich." *The New York Times* (New York), August 4, 1985, sec. 23, p. 20.

The Harcus Gallery, Boston, Massachusetts.
Jungle Fever,
September 7-October 2.

Stapen, Nancy. "'Jungle Fever' show mirrors modern artists' concerns." *The Boston Herald* (Boston), September 22, 1985, Arts & Entertainment Section, p. 30.

Temin, Christine. "'Jungle Fever' show makes a fun adventure." *The Boston Globe* (Boston), September 26, 1985, Arts and Film section, p. 76.

San Antonio Art Institute, Texas.
Texas Currents,
September 26-October 31.
Catalogue text by Howard Smagula.

Goddard, Dan R. "New 'Currents' in Texas Art." *Express-News* (San Antonio), September 29, 1985, sec. H, pp. 12, 13.

Solon, Marcia Goren. "'Currents' doesn't have needed pull." *San Antonio Light* (San Antonio), October 6, 1985, sec. P, pp. 1, 7.

Goddard, Dan R. "Artist one of Texas' 'Currents'." *Express-News* (San Antonio), October 20, 1985, sec. H, p. 6.

Fisch, Carol. "The State of the Art of the State." *San Antonio Monthly* (San Antonio), vol. 5, no. 1, October 1985, pp. 48-51.

Goddard, Dan R. "Texas Currents." *Artspace* (Albuquerque), vol. 10, no. 1, Winter 1985-86, pp. 22-25.

Shukalo, Alice. "'Texas Currents' in San Antonio." *Texas Journal* (Dallas), vol. 8, no. 1, Fall-Winter 1985-86, pp. 42, 43.

1986   Texas Gallery, Houston.
Texas Group Show,
January 7-February 1.

Minneapolis College of Art and Design, Minnesota.
A Sense of Place: Contemporary Southern Art,
January 31-March 14.
Catalogue text by Eleanor Heartney.

Hirshhorn Museum and Sculpture Garden, Washington, D.C.
Directions 1986,
February 6-March 30.
Catalogue text by Phyllis Rosenzweig.

Richard, Paul. "'Directions': Up and Down." *Washington Post* (Washington, D.C.), February 8, 1986, sec. C, pp. 1, 7.

Allen, Jane Addams. "Exhibiting an Absence of Judgment." *Washington Times* (Washington, D.C.), February 24, 1986, Capital Life section, pp. 72, 73.

Lawrence, Leone. "Reviews, Washington, D.C.: Directions 1986." *ARTnews* (New York), vol. 85, no. 4, April 1986, pp. 144, 145.

McIntosh/Drysdale Gallery, Washington, D.C.
Five Texas Artists,
March 5-April 12.

Lewis, Jo Ann. "The Texas Trend." *The Washington Post* (Washington, D.C.), March 8, 1986, sec. C, p. 2.

Tilden-Foley Gallery, New Orleans.
Texas!,
March 22-April 19.
Catalogue, *State of The Art: Texas!,* produced by the Contemporary Arts Center, New Orleans.

Green, Roger. "Group show of Texas artists impressive, challenging effort." *The Times-Picayune* (New Orleans), March 30, 1986, sec. C, p. 8.

The Museum of Fine Arts, Houston.
The Texas Landscape, 1900-1986,
May 17-September 7.
Catalogue text by Susie Kalil.

The Brooklyn Museum, New York.
The Third Western States Biennial Exhibition,
June 6-August 5.
Catalogue text by Charlotta Kotik.
Traveling to New Orleans Contemporary Art Center, September 27-November 8; Colorado Springs Fine Arts Center, Colorado, March 14-May 17, 1987; San Antonio Museum of Art, Texas, June 7-July 24, 1987; Yellowstone Fine Arts Center, Billings, Montana, August 9-October 10, 1987, Palm Springs Desert Museum, California, November 20, 1987-January 10, 1988; San José Museum of Art, California, February 5-April 3, 1988.

Arranged chronologically.

1981 Kalil, Susie. "Survey of Texas Art: Melissa Miller." *Arts and Architecture* (Los Angeles), vol. 1, no. 2, Winter 1981, pp. 26, 27.

1982 Taliaferro, John. "Melissa's Ark." *Third Coast* (Austin), vol. 1, no. 11, June 1982, pp. 64-67.

Freudenheim, Susan. "Uniting art and allegory: the energetic paintings of Melissa Miller." *Texas Homes* (Dallas), vol. 6, no. 6, July 1982, pp. 23, 24, 26.

Tucker, Marcia. "An Iconography of Recent Figurative Painting: Sex, Death, Violence, and the Apocalypse." *Artforum* (New York), vol. 20, no. 10, Summer 1982, pp. 70-75.

Vander Lee, Jana. "Texas Art, Hot and Heavy." *Artspace* (Albuquerque), vol. 6, no. 4, Fall 1982, pp. 8-10.

1983 Russell, John. "It's Not 'Women's Art,' It's Good Art." *The New York Times* (New York), July 24, 1983, sec. 2, pp. 1, 25.

1984 Johnson, Patricia C. "MFA Plans Exciting Year." *Houston Chronicle* (Houston), May 16, 1984, sec. 3, pp. 1, 5.

Wolff, Theodore F. "On Not Taking Nature for Granted; The Many Masks of Modern Art." *The Christian Science Monitor* (Boston), June 21, 1984, p. 34.

Brenson, Michael. "Animals Creep Back Into Today's Art." *The New York Times* (New York), June 24, 1984, sec. H, pp. 27, 29.

Derrickson, Steve. "Miller's Menagerie Unleashed." *Austin Chronicle* (Austin), vol. 3, no. 25, August 10, 1984, p. 12.

Russell, John. "American Art Gains New Energies." *The New York Times* (New York), August 19, 1984, sec. 2, pp. 1, 18.

Feinstein, Roni. "Melissa Miller: The Uses of Enchantment." *Arts Magazine* (New York), vol. 58, no. 10, Summer 1984, pp. 70-72.

Colacello, Bob. "Voices of Houston." *Vanity Fair* (New York), vol. 47, no. 10, October 1984, p. 86.

Freeman, Phyllis. *New Art.* New York: Harry N. Abrams, 1984.

1985 Gardner, Ralph Jr. "Turning Points: Women Talk About Decisions That Changed Their Lives." *Cosmopolitan* (New York), vol. 198, no. 3, March 1985, pp. 240-244.

Rose, Barbara. "Rule Breakers." *Vogue* (New York), vol. 175, no. 6, June 1985, pp. 246-251.

Barac, Jean Williams. "Art's Rising Star." *Austin Magazine* (Austin), vol. 27, no. 3, July 1985, pp. 93, 94.

Articles and Books

Moser, Charlotte. "Regional Revisions: Houston and Chicago." *Art in America* (New York), vol. 73, no. 7, July 1985, pp. 90-99.

Kaufman, Charles. "Melissa Miller's on a roll." *Austin American-Statesman* (Austin), October 1, 1985, Onward section, pp. cover, 16-18.

Sasser, Elizabeth Skidmore. "Dogs of the Golden West." *Southwest Art* (Houston), vol. 15, no. 6, November 1985, pp. 84-92.

Lucie-Smith, Edward. *American Art Now.* New York: William Morrow and Company, Inc., 1985.

1986 Kane, Karen. "Three Texas Artists: The Contemporary Arts Museum Celebrates the Sesqui-centennial." *Houston Chronicle* (Houston), January 12, 1986, Magazine section. pp. 5-7.

Tackett, Helen. "Huntington Gallery adds 44 paintings to collection." *On Campus* (The University of Texas at Austin), vol. 13, no. 17, January 27-February 2, 1986, p. 13.

Becker, Robert. "Art in View." *Interview* (New York), vol. 14, no. 3, March 1986, pp. 166, 167.

Ottman, Klaus. "Who Paints Abstractly? Blinky Palermo and Melissa Miller." *Flash Art* (Milan), no. 126, February/March 1986, p. 47.

Brenson, Michael. "Why Asian Culture Answers the Needs of Western Artists." *The New York Times* (New York), April 20, 1986, sec. 2, pp. 31, 34.

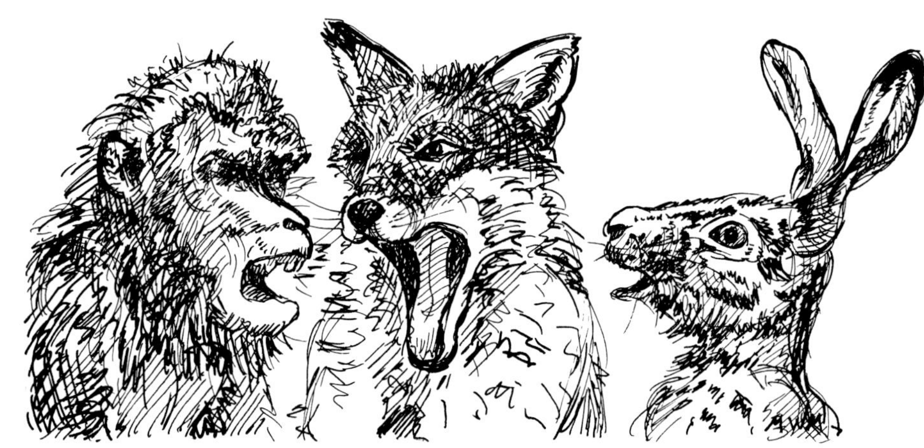

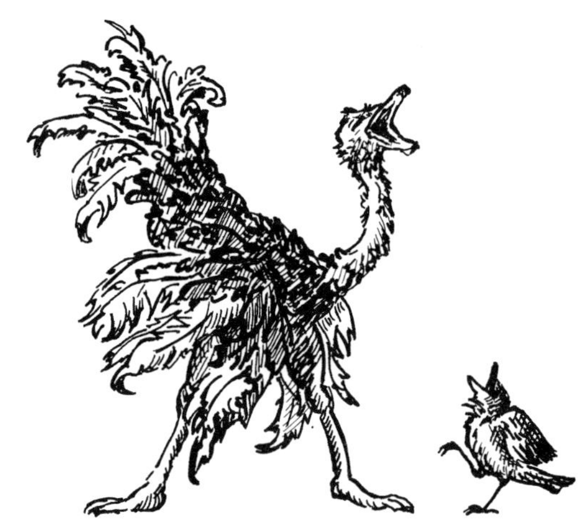

Photograph credits

Julie Bozzi, pp. 47 *(bottom)*, 52 *(bottom)*. Dennis Bradbury, p. 57 *(top)*. John Dyer, p. 39 *(top)*. James Flannery, pp. 43 *(bottom)*, 47 *(top)*. Rick Gardner • Houston, pp. 36 *(bottom)*, 37 *(top)*, 43 *(top)*, 56 *(left)*, 58 *(top)*, 62 *(top)*, 66 *(top)*, 69, 73, 74, 75 *(top and middle)*, 77. Hickey-Robertson, p. 28. © Bill Kennedy, pp. 36 *(top)*, 37 *(bottom)*, 38, 39 *(bottom)*, 40, 41, 42, 44, 45, 46, 48 *(bottom)*, 49, 50, 51, 52 *(top)*, 53 *(top)*, 54, 55, 57 *(bottom)*, 59, 60, 61, 63, 66 *(bottom)*, 67, 68, 70, 71, 72, 75 *(bottom)*, 76. Robert Mapplethorpe, p. 78. Skeet McAuley, p. 53 *(bottom)*. Pelka/Noble Photography, p. 64 *(left)*. Adam Reich, pp. 48 *(top)*, 58 *(bottom)*, 62 *(bottom)*. Lee Stalsworth, p. 64 *(right)*. Tom Van Eynde, p. 56 *(right)*.

Cover and text illustrations by Melissa Miller, 1986
Typesetting by Characters, Inc.
5000 copies printed by Wetmore & Co.
Distributed nationally by the Contemporary Arts Museum and Texas Monthly Press